The stolen heiress or the Salamanca doctor outplotted. A comedy. As it is acted at the New Theatre in Lincolns-Inn-Fields. By Her Majesties servants.

Susanna Centlivre

Eighteenth Century
Collections Online
Print Editions

Gale ECCO Print Editions

Relive history with *Eighteenth Century Collections Online*, now available in print for the independent historian and collector. This series includes the most significant English-language and foreign-language works printed in Great Britain during the eighteenth century, and is organized in seven different subject areas including literature and language; medicine, science, and technology; and religion and philosophy. The collection also includes thousands of important works from the Americas.

The eighteenth century has been called "The Age of Enlightenment." It was a period of rapid advance in print culture and publishing, in world exploration, and in the rapid growth of science and technology – all of which had a profound impact on the political and cultural landscape. At the end of the century the American Revolution, French Revolution and Industrial Revolution, perhaps three of the most significant events in modern history, set in motion developments that eventually dominated world political, economic, and social life.

In a groundbreaking effort, Gale initiated a revolution of its own: digitization of epic proportions to preserve these invaluable works in the largest online archive of its kind. Contributions from major world libraries constitute over 175,000 original printed works. Scanned images of the actual pages, rather than transcriptions, recreate the works ***as they first appeared.***

Now for the first time, these high-quality digital scans of original works are available via print-on-demand, making them readily accessible to libraries, students, independent scholars, and readers of all ages.

For our initial release we have created seven robust collections to form one the world's most comprehensive catalogs of 18th century works.

Initial Gale ECCO Print Editions collections include:

History and Geography
Rich in titles on English life and social history, this collection spans the world as it was known to eighteenth-century historians and explorers. Titles include a wealth of travel accounts and diaries, histories of nations from throughout the world, and maps and charts of a world that was still being discovered. Students of the War of American Independence will find fascinating accounts from the British side of conflict.

Social Science
Delve into what it was like to live during the eighteenth century by reading the first-hand accounts of everyday people, including city dwellers and farmers, businessmen and bankers, artisans and merchants, artists and their patrons, politicians and their constituents. Original texts make the American, French, and Industrial revolutions vividly contemporary.

Medicine, Science and Technology
Medical theory and practice of the 1700s developed rapidly, as is evidenced by the extensive collection, which includes descriptions of diseases, their conditions, and treatments. Books on science and technology, agriculture, military technology, natural philosophy, even cookbooks, are all contained here.

Literature and Language
Western literary study flows out of eighteenth-century works by Alexander Pope, Daniel Defoe, Henry Fielding, Frances Burney, Denis Diderot, Johann Gottfried Herder, Johann Wolfgang von Goethe, and others. Experience the birth of the modern novel, or compare the development of language using dictionaries and grammar discourses.

Religion and Philosophy
The Age of Enlightenment profoundly enriched religious and philosophical understanding and continues to influence present-day thinking. Works collected here include masterpieces by David Hume, Immanuel Kant, and Jean-Jacques Rousseau, as well as religious sermons and moral debates on the issues of the day, such as the slave trade. The Age of Reason saw conflict between Protestantism and Catholicism transformed into one between faith and logic -- a debate that continues in the twenty-first century.

Law and Reference
This collection reveals the history of English common law and Empire law in a vastly changing world of British expansion. Dominating the legal field is the *Commentaries of the Law of England* by Sir William Blackstone, which first appeared in 1765. Reference works such as almanacs and catalogues continue to educate us by revealing the day-to-day workings of society.

Fine Arts
The eighteenth-century fascination with Greek and Roman antiquity followed the systematic excavation of the ruins at Pompeii and Herculaneum in southern Italy; and after 1750 a neoclassical style dominated all artistic fields. The titles here trace developments in mostly English-language works on painting, sculpture, architecture, music, theater, and other disciplines. Instructional works on musical instruments, catalogs of art objects, comic operas, and more are also included.

The BiblioLife Network

This project was made possible in part by the BiblioLife Network (BLN), a project aimed at addressing some of the huge challenges facing book preservationists around the world. The BLN includes libraries, library networks, archives, subject matter experts, online communities and library service providers. We believe every book ever published should be available as a high-quality print reproduction; printed on-demand anywhere in the world. This insures the ongoing accessibility of the content and helps generate sustainable revenue for the libraries and organizations that work to preserve these important materials.

The following book is in the "public domain" and represents an authentic reproduction of the text as printed by the original publisher. While we have attempted to accurately maintain the integrity of the original work, there are sometimes problems with the original work or the micro-film from which the books were digitized. This can result in minor errors in reproduction. Possible imperfections include missing and blurred pages, poor pictures, markings and other reproduction issues beyond our control. Because this work is culturally important, we have made it available as part of our commitment to protecting, preserving, and promoting the world's literature.

GUIDE TO FOLD-OUTS MAPS and OVERSIZED IMAGES

The book you are reading was digitized from microfilm captured over the past thirty to forty years. Years after the creation of the original microfilm, the book was converted to digital files and made available in an online database.

In an online database, page images do not need to conform to the size restrictions found in a printed book. When converting these images back into a printed bound book, the page sizes are standardized in ways that maintain the detail of the original. For large images, such as fold-out maps, the original page image is split into two or more pages

Guidelines used to determine how to split the page image follows:

• Some images are split vertically; large images require vertical and horizontal splits.
• For horizontal splits, the content is split left to right.
• For vertical splits, the content is split from top to bottom.
• For both vertical and horizontal splits, the image is processed from top left to bottom right.

THE
STOLEN HEIRESS
OR THE
Salamanca Doctor Outplotted.
A
COMEDY.

As it is Acted at the New Theatre in *Lincolns-Inn-Fields.*

BY
Her Majesties Servants.

Nihil dictum quod non ante dictum.

LONDON,

Printed for *William Turner* at the Angel at *Lincolns-Inn-Back Gate*, and *John Nutt* near *Stationers-Hall*. Price 1 s. 6 d.

☞ Lately Printed *She Wou'd and She Wou'd not*, a Comedy, Written by Mr. *Cibber*. Price 1 s. 6 d. Sold by *William Turner* and *John Nutt*.

To the Honourable

Sir *STAFFORD FAIRBORN,*

Rear Admiral of the White

SIR,

IF our Laws and Liberties be dear to us, how much are we indebted to those by whom they are secured, and 'tis the duty of every gratefull person in some measure to pay their acknowment, to such whose Care and Courage protects them from the rude insults of Arbitrary Power, among which none is more Conspicuous than your self

What you have done for *England's* safety shows the great Stock from whence you sprung, your Noble Father, whose Glorious Actions will to Posterity record his Name whilst you, his Son, pursue his Glorious steps, and guard your Country from invading Foes, a subject for Incomiums from our abler Pens, for what can like Poetry preserve a brave Man's Fame, the greatest Conqueror the World

The Epistle Dedicatory.

ere knew, but for that had in Oblivion flept, and the *Grecian* Hero receiv'd more lasting Glory from the blind Bards Immortal Lines, than did *Egyptian* Monarchs, whose insatiate thirst for eternal Fame errected Piramids of prodigious bulk, strong and durable, as they thought the World it self. Yet these, and Statues too of Stone and Brass are now devour'd by the Iron teeth of Time, and not so much as the Founders Name left undefac'd, but Poets give eternal life to great Exploits, which thro variety of Languages gain universal Praise.

I am proud to be the first that in this kind have laid an Offering at your Feet, thereby shewing our greatest wits a subject worthy their sublimest thoughts, for tho the Poet makes the Verse, 'tis the Hero makes the Poet.

Your Conduct, Bravery and Success at Sea shows you were born for War, and justly chosen to Command a Fleet, that does Command the World, yet is not your Courage more terrible to your Enemies abroad than your courteous affability, and obliging condescention is charming to your friends at home.

The Muse still studies to pay her earliest tribute to the most deserving, and in all her search, where can she find Merit more than yours, alured by these thoughts she Courts your Protection, a Protection that wou'd make even Cowards loose their Fear, and by your bright Example straight grow Valiant, you'l excuse I hope, Sir, the zeal that hurried me

on

The Epistle Dedicatory.

on to make this small Essay in your Praise, and my Countries Honour, 'tis daring I confess in one who is unqualified for a Theme so ample: But fear being a Vice you ever hated, I may presume to be more easily pardon'd for this bold attempt, and allow'd to lay hold of this opportunity of declaring to the World how much I am,

SIR,

Your Most Faithfull,

Most Obedient,

And most Humble Servant.

A SONG designed to be Sung by Mr. *Dogget.*

THE Man you Ladies ought to fear,
  Behold and see his Picture here,
With Arms a cross and down-cast Eyes
Thus languishes, and thus he dies,
Then gives his Hat a careless pull,
Thus high, and thus looks dull,
Thus he sighs, thus he swears,
Thus he turns, and thus he tears.
This, this, is he you can move,
And this the Man the Ladies love.

PROLOGUE,
Spoke by Mrs PRINCE.

Our Author fearing his success to day,
Sends me to bribe your Spleen against his Play,
And if a Ghost in Nelly's time cou'd sooth ye,
He hopes in these that Flesh and Blood may move ye.
Nay, what is more, to win your hearts, a Maid!
If ever such a thing the Play-House had.
For cold and shade the waxen Blossom's born,
Not to endure the Regions of the Sun,
Let every Beau then his applause begin,
And think the rarity was born for him:
Your true bred Knights for fancy'd Dames advance,
And think it Gallanty to break a Launce,
And shall a real Damsel e're be found
To plead her Cause in vain on English ground,
Unless that dreadful Prophecy's began,
In which Seven Women are to share———one Man!
But thanks my Stars, that danger I disown,
For in the Pit, I see 'tis———one — to one.
And while the Fair can all their rights enjoy,
We'll keep our Title up to being Coy,
So let your Praise be noisy as your Wine,
And grant your Favours, if you'd purchase mine

Dramatis Personæ.

Governour	Of *Palermo*.	Mr. *Bowman*.
Count Pirro	Nephew to the Governour.	Mr. *Griffith*.
Gravello	A *Sicilian* Lord Father to *Lucasia*.	Mr. *Freeman*.
Larich	His Brother.	Mr. *Fieldhouse*.
Lord Euphenes	An old *Secilian* General.	Mr. *Arnold*.
Palante	Son to *Euphenes* but unknown in Love with *Lucasia*.	Mr. *Powel*.
Clerimont	His Friend.	Mr. *Baile*.
Eugenio	Son to *Gravello* in disguise under the name of *Iras*.	Mr. *Booth*.
Alphonso	Formerly an Officer under *Euphenes*.	Mr. *Knap*.
Francisco	In Love with *Lavinia*.	Mr. *Pack*.
Sancho	A Pedant bred at *Salamanca*, designed by *Larich* a Husband for *Lavinia*.	Mr. *Dogget*.
Tristram	His Man.	Mr. *Lee*.
Rosco	Servant to *Count Gravello*.	Mr. *Bright*.

WOMEN.

Lucasia.	Daughter to *Gravello*, in Love with *Palante*.	Mrs. *Barry*.
Lavinia	Daughter to *Larich*, in Love with *Francisco*.	Mrs. *Prince*.
Laura	Woman to *Lucasia*.	Mrs. *Lawson*.

The SCENE *Palermo*.

THE HEIRESS:

OR, THE

Salamanca DOCTOR Out-plotted.

ACT I.
SCENE I.

Enter Count Grovello *and* Rosco.

Gra. Rosco!

Rosco. My Lord.

Gra. Hast thou divulg'd the News that my Son died at *Rome*?

Rosco. Yes, my Lord, with every Circumstance, the Time, the Place, and manner of his Death; that 'tis believed, and

told

to'd for truth with as much confidence, as they had been Spectators of his End.

Gra. That's well, that's very well, now *Rosco* follows my part, I must express a most unusual grief, not like a well-left Heir for his dead Father, or a lusty Widdow for an old decripit Husband; no, I must counterfeit in a far deeper strain; weep like a Parent for an only Son: Is not this a hard task? Ha, *Rosco*?

Rosco. Ah, no, my Lord, not for your Skill; in your Youth your Lordship saw Plays, convers'd with Players, knew the fam'd *Alberto*

Gra. 'Tis true, by Heav'n, I have seen that Knave paint Grief in such a lively colour, that for false and acted Passion he has drawn true Tears, the Ladies kept time with his Sighs, and wept to his sad Accents as he had truly been the Man he seem'd, then I'll try my part, thou has't still been privy to my Bosom; secrets know'st Wealth, and Ambition are the Darlings of my Soul; nor will I leave a Stratagem unessay'd to raise my Family. My Son is well and safe, but by Command from me he returns not this three Months. My Daughter, my *Lucasia*, is my only care, and to advance her Fortune, have I fram'd this Project; how dost like it *Rosco*, ha?

Rosco. Rarely, my Lord, my Lady will be now suppos'd the Heir to all your vast Revenues, and pester'd with more Suitors than the *Grecian* Queen, in the long absence of her Lord. You'll have the Dons, Lords and Dukes swarm about your House like Bees.

Gra. My aim is fixt at the Rich and Great, he that has Wealth enough, yet longs for more, Count *Pirro*, the Governour's Heir and Nephew, that rich Lord that knows no end of his large Fortunes, yet still gapes on, for Gold is a sure Bait to gain him, no other Loadstone can attrack his iron heart, 'tis proof against the force of Beauty, else I should not need this Stratagem, for Nature has not prov'd a Nigard to my Daughter.

Rosco.

Rosco. To him, I'm sure, she's play'd the Step-Dame, I much fear *Lucasia* will not relish such a Match.

Gra Ha! not relish it! has she any other Taft but mine, or shall she dare to wish ought that may contradict my purpose--- But hold, perhaps you know how she's inclin'd, you may be Confederate with her, and manage her Intreagues with that Begger *Palante*, who is only by Lord *Exphane's* bounty, my mortal Enemies, kept from starving

Ros. Who I, my good Lord? Heav'n knows, I have learnt by your Lordship's Example, always to hate the Poor, and like the Courtier, never to do ought without a Bribe.

Enter a Servant.

Serv. My Lord, Count *Pirro*, to wait upon your Lordship.

Gra. Conduct him in. [*Exit* Serv] Now *Rosco*, to my Couch; if my Plot takes, I'm a happy Man.

Enter Count Pirro.

Pirro. Is your Lord asleep?

Ros I think not, my Lord, but thus he lies, Heav'n knows when this grief will end--- My Lord, my Lord, the Count of *Pirro*.

Gra. I pray your Lordship pardon me, at this time I'm not fit to entertain Persons of your Worth.

Pir Alass! my Lord, I know your grief

Ros. Ay, 'twas that brought his good Lordship hither.

Pirro. You have lost a worthy, and a hopeful Son, but Heav'n that always gives, will sometimes take, and there is no Balsam left to cure these Wounds but patience; there's no disputing with it, yet if there were, in what could you ac-

cuse

cute those Pow'rs, that else have been so liberal to you, and left you yet to bless your Age a beauteous Daughter.

Ros. Now it begins to work, (*aside*)

Pirro. Your Blood is not Extinct, nor are you Childless, Sir, from that fair Branch may come much fruit to glad posterity: think on this, my Lord.

Gra. I know I should not repine, my Lord, but nature will prevail, I cannot help reflecting on my Loss; alas, my Lord, you know not what it is to lose a Son; 'tis true, I have still a Child, Heav'n has now confin'd my care to one, to see her well bestow'd shall be the business of my Life —— Oh! my *Eugenio*

Ros. Egad, he does it rarely, (*aside.*)

Pirro. How shall I manage, that he may not suspect my love to his Daughter proceeds from his Son's death, (*aside.*) I was just coming to make a Proposal to your Lordship as the News reach'd my Ear, I much fear the time's improper now to talk of business

Gra. Pray Heav'n it be the business I wish; were my grief more great, if possible, yet would I suspend it to hear, my Lord, of *Pirro*.

Ros. Cunningly insinuated, (*aside*)

Pirro. Your Lordship is too obliging.

Gra. Not at all, pray proceed, my Lord.

Pirro. It was, my Lord, to have ask't the fair *Lucasia* for my Wife

Ros. So he has swallow'd the bait, (*aside*)

Gra. As I could wish, (*aside*)

Pirro. 'Twas not out of any Consideration of her present Fortune, my Lord, I hope you'l not believe, since I design'd it e're I knew *Eugenio* dead I wish he may believe me, (*aside.*)

Gra. If 'twas, my Lord of *Pirro* does deserve it all, nor would I wish my Child a better Match. But 'tis too soon to treat of Marriage after such a Loss.

Rosco.

Rosco. Dear Sir, consent to this good Lord, so will your care be over, and hopeful Grandsons make up poor *Eugenio*'s loss.

Gra. What, would you have me think of Joy and Death at once, and mingle the Grave and Marriages together.

Pirro If you'll consent, my Lord, a private Marriage may be had, and so dispence with the usual Solemnities of Joy. If you refuse me, I shall think you slight my Claim.

Gra. That Argument alone prevails. No, I will never give the Count of *Pirro* cause to doubt of my Esteem.

Ros. Consider, my Lord, she's an Heiress, that may set bold, desperate Youths on rash Attempts; and tho' they know *Sicilian* Laws gives death to him that steals an Heiress, yet I'll not warrant her Safety till to morrow night.

Pirro He's in the right, my Lord.

Gra Away, and call her, tho' she's disorder'd with her Griefs. Now thou hast rais'd another Fear, and my poor heart trembles for *Lucasia*, as it for *Eugenio* bleeds. (*Ex* Rosco.

Pirro. Within my arms she shall be safe and happy, the Governour, my noble Uncle, and my Friend, her great Protector.

Enter Rosco *with* Lucasia.

Gra, Come near *Lucasia,* like the Ambassadors from this World's great Rulers, I bring the Grief and Joy, pause not upon a Brother's Loss, tho' 'twas a dear one; but fix thy thoughts here, upon this Lord, thus I bequeath thee to the illustrious Count of *Pirro*

Pirro Thus I with extasy receive her,
   [*Kneels and kisses her hand.*

Luc. You'll give me leave, my Lord, to wake from this Con-
Is't possible! do I behold my Father?   (fusion:
Can he resolve, at once, to part with both
His Children, my Brother, the best of Men,
No more will bless his Roof, no more will grace

This Pallace with his presence----
Must I be cast out too, far more unblest
Than he whose lodg'd within the peaceful Grave.
Oh, send me to him, e're you condemn me
T'perpetual Bondage, to a life of woe;
To a Marriage unthought of, unforeseen.

Pirro Madam----

Gra. Mind her not, my Lord, 'tis grief, 'tis mere distraction, she shan't dispute my Will Please to walk in, my Lord, we'll peruse the Writings of your Estate, and hear what Settlement you'll make her, and to morrow the Priest shall join you, to aleviate her Griefs, and Mind.

Pirro. But to see her weep thus damps all my rising joy.

Gra They are but Virgin Tears, pray come withme, Daughter, you know my Will, I expect you be Obedient; you know 'tis your Duty.

Luc. I know 'tis, Sir.----
But you, I hope, will give my tortur'd Heart
Your leave to break, and that may shew my Duty.

Pirro. Fair *Lucasia.*

Luc Oh, Distraction!   [*Flings from him.*]

Gra. Pray come, my Lord, let her have her way, the fits of Women's grief last not long, at least when I command she shall Obey.

                      [*Exeunt* all but *Lucasia*]

Luc. A dismal Sentence, it strikes me upon my Soul,
And raises Terrors far more grim than Death;
Forgive me, Brother, if t'thy Memory
I pay not one Tear more, all now are due
To Love, and my *Palante.*

                                       Enter

Enter Laura.

Lau. You name the Man that waits by me conceal'd,
For one blest Minute to comfort his *Lucasia*.
  Luc. All Minutes now are Curst, no chearful day,
Will ever bring the lost *Lucasia* Peace.
  Lau. Come forth, Sir, I believe you'l prove the best Physician.

Enter Palante.

  Luc. Oh *Palante*, art thou come prepar'd to weep,
Else, for me, thou art no fit Companion,
For I have News will rack thy very Soul.
  Pal. Yes, I have heard of brave *Eugenio*'s death;
He was thy Brother, and my early Friend:
Thus doubly ty'd, thou need'st not doubt I mourn
Him truly-----
  Luc. Oh poor *Palante*!
So wretched *Alcione* did at distance grieve,
When she beheld the floating Corps,
And knew not 'twas her Husband.
  Pal. What means my Love?
  Luc. Dost thou not love me, my *Palante*?
  Pal. Oh! after so many Years of faithful Service,
Why am I ask'd that Question?
  Luc. It were better that thou didst not, for when
Thou hear'st the Story 'twill turn thee into Marble;
'Twill shock thy manly heart, and make each Nerve
Loose its accustomed Faculty, chill all
Thy Blood, and make thine Eyes run o're like mine,
For we must part for ever.

Pal.

Lu. Can that Voice pronounce a sound so dreadful?
Art thou then alter'd with thy fortune? Must
I lose thee.

   Luc. O thou unkind one to suspect my Love,
My promis'd Faith, or think me in the least
Consenting to my rigid Father's Will,
Who, but now has given me to the Count of *Pirro*

   Pa. Ha! to the Count of *Pirro*, that lump of Deformity
My Sword has been my fortune hitherto,
And ne're was wont to fail its Master, and
Whilst this Arm can hold it, I'll maintain my Right

   Luc. Which way rash Man, is he not surrounded
By numerous Friends, and waiting Slaves?
Does not inevitable Death attend
Thy desperate purpose?

   Pal. Then let that same Sword, the old acquaintance
Of my Arm, pierce its lost Master's breast, and
End my Sorrows.

   Luc. Forbid it Heaven, is there no other way?

   Pal But one, and that I dare not name.

   Luc. Oh! how has thy *Lucasia*, since first our
Mutual Vows were plighted, given Cause for doubt.
Why dost thou fear to ask, since all is thine, within
The Bounds of Honour

   Pal When I attempt ought against *Lucasia*.
Contrary to the nicest Rules of Virtue,
May Heaven, and she, forsake.

   Luc. Oh, I know it, and when I refuse what
May advance our Loves, may I be Curst
With that hatred Count of *Pirro*. Speak, my *Palante*,

   Pal. Can I ----- Ye all-seeing Powers, move so bold a Suit,
Oh! let me humbly ask it on my knees,
To quit her cruel Father's house,
And all the Grandeur of a pompous Court.

                                        To

To bear a part in my hard Fortunes;
Oh! 'tis too much to think, to wish, to hope.

 Luc. Yes, dear *Palante*, more than this I'de do
For thee,
What's Pomp and Greatness, when compar'd with Love?
Oh! that thou wert some humble Shepherd on
Our *Sicilian* Plain, I thy chearful Mate
Wou'd, watch with pleasure till the Ev'ning tyde,
And wait thy blest return, with as much joy
As Queens expect Victorious Monarchs, and
Think my self more blest than they. But, oh *Palante!*
Thou knowst our Country's Laws gives Death without
Reprieve, to him that Weds an Heiress against her Parents Will,
Tho' with her own Consent.

 Pal. Who would not Dye to purchase thee? For I
Must Dye without thee.

 Luc. No, live *Palante*, we'll together tread
The Maze of life, and stand the shock of Fate.
The Power's Decree, or both our happiness,
Or both our miseries, where shall we meet?
For I will leave this loathsom House, before their
Watch grows stricter.

 Pal. Will thou then forsake the World for thy *Palante*?
Everlasting Blessings fall around thee,
And Crown thy Days and Nights with peace and joy.
Oh! my fond heart, I cannot half express
The Raptures thou hast rais'd, thou Treasure of
My Soul, let me Embrace thee, and while thus
I hold thee in my arms, I'm richer than
The *Eastern* Monarch, nor wou'd I quit thee
To be as Great as he-----
Oh! let but what my Arms infolds be mine;
Take all the rest the World contains, my Life.

 Luc. My *Palante*-----

C

Pal.

Pal. I have an only Friend, faithful and just,
As Men of Old before Deceit became
A Trade, he shall assist us in our flight;
He shall prepare a Priest, if thou wilt meet
Me in the *Eastern* Grove; when we are Wed
We'll fly to *Spain*, till Time and Friends procure
My Pardon.

    Luc. In some disguise I'le meet thee there,
Just at the hour of Noon,
For then my Father sleeps, and I will take
The opportunity——
And, oh! I fear no danger but for thee.

    Pal. For me there's none, whilst thou'rt safe, and with me
Thy loss alone can make *Palante* dye.

Enter Laura.

Laura. Madam, your Father——
Luc. Away *Palante*, may all the Powr's preserve thee.
Pal. And thou the best of Woman-kind.
                                        [*Exeunt severally.*

Lucas. O Love, thou that hast join'd a faithful Pair,
    Guard my Palante, make him all thy care.
    Fate's utmost rigour we resolve to try,
    Live both together, or together Dye.

Enter Count Gravello, Larich *and* Lavinia.

    Gra. Brother, you are welcome to the House of Sorrow; but I have learnt so much Philosophy, to cease to Mourn when the Cause is past redress. Once more, forgetting Grief, you are welcome, you, and my fair Neice.
                                              Larich.

Larich. Thank you Brother---- the Girl's a foolish Girl--- Marriageable, but foolish--- You understand me.

Lavin. I thank you, Sir.

Larich. Why, are you not a Fool, Hussy-- look y'Brother, I have provided the Mynx a rich Husband, a Scholar too, Body of me bred all his Youth at *Salamanca*, learn'd enough to commence Doctor--- I love a learned Man, especially when Riches too concur; he is the Son and Heir of my old Friend *Don Sancho* of *Syracuse*---- and the Baggage cry's *I hate him*, and yet has never seen him; but she is in Love, forsooth, with a young beggarly Dog, not worth a Groat, but I'll prevent her, I'll warrant her.

Gra. Just, just my Case, we are Brothers in every thing, my Daughter too thinks her judgment wisest, and flies a Fortune for a Princess, but her reign's at an end, to morrow I'm rid of her; I warrant you, Brother, we'll hamper the young Sluts.

Lavin. You may be both mistaken, old Gentlemen,
If my Cousin is of my mind.

Larich. What's that you mutter, Mrs. *Littlewit*

Lavin. I say, I long to see my Cousin *Lucasia*, Sir, I hope that's no Crime.

Gra. No, no, *Rosco*, wait of her in to my Daughter, and dost hear *Lavinia*? Preethy let Obedience be thy study, and teach it her.

Lavin. I'll warrant you, Sir, I'll teach her to be Obedient, if she'll but follow my advice, (*aside*) but 'tis something hard, tho' Uncle, to Marry a Man at first sight, one's heard but an indifferent Character of

Larich. How, Hussy, are you a Judge of Characters? Is he not a Scholar? Answer me that.

Lavin. A meer Scholar is a meer--- You know the old Proverb, Father.

Larich. Do you hear the perverse Baggage; get you out of my sight, Hussy.

Lavin. I am obedient, Sir,--- I dare swear I shall find better Company, than two old arbitrary Dons.

[*Exit with* Rosco.

Larich. Did you ever see such a Slut? body a'me these wild Wenches are enough to make old Men mad.

Gra. My Daughter is of another Strain, solid as Man, but obstinate as Woman; but no matter when she is married my care is over, let Count *Pirro* look to't.

Larich Count *Pirro!* body o'me a mighty Fortune for my Cousin; why, he's rich enough to buy a Principality; my Son's rich too, and a great Scholar, which I admire above all things.

Enter Rosco.

Rosco. Oh! Sir, such News, such a Sight, Sir!

Larich. What's the matter.

Rosco. Don Sancho come to Town in his *Salamanca* habit, his Dress, and grave Phiz has alarm'd the Mobb, that there's such a Crowd about the Inn door, I'le maintain't his Landlord gives him free Quarter for a Twelve-Month, if he'l let him expose him to advantage, ha, ha, ha, he makes as odd a Figure, Sir, as the famous *Don Quixot*, when he went in search of his *Dulcinea*.

Larich. Brother, pray Correct your Servant, I like not his rediculous Jests upon the Habit of the Learned, my Son-in-Law that is to be, minds nothing but his Books.

Rosco.

Rosco. Sir, I ask your pardon, my nigard Stars have not allow'd line enough to my Judgment, to fathom the profundity of your Son's shallow Capacity--- (*lowing Comically.*

Gra. Peace, Sirrah--- Come, Brother, now your Son's arriv'd, I hope we shall have a double Match to morrow,---- We'll not consult the Women, but force them to their Happiness,

Experienc'd Age knows what for Youth is fit;
With wise Men, Wealth, out-weighs both Parts and Wit.

[Exeunt.]

ACT

ACT II.

Scene I. *Lucasia's* Chamber.

Enter Lucasia *and* Lavinia.

Lavi. UPon my life, Cousin, I think my Condition worse than yours, and yet you see I am not so much dejected.

Luca. Oh! What Condition is't can equal mine?
Much less exceed it; to be oblig'd to
Break my Vow, to part from my *Palante*;
Forc'd to the Arms of a mishap'en Monster,
Whom Nature made to vex the whole Creation.
Nor is his crooked Body more deform'd
Than is his Soul, Ambition is his God;
He seeks no Heav'n but Interest, nor knows he
How to value ought but Gold.
Oh! my dearest Brother, had'st thou but liv'd
I had been truly happy, but now am
Doubly miserable, in losing thee, and my *Palante*

Lavi. For Heav'ns sake, don't afflict your self at this rate, but study rather to avoid the Ill, if you would Counter-plot my Uncle; dry up your Eyes, and let the Woman work, I warrant you may contrive some way to get rid of this lump of Worms-meat; I don't fear giving my Father the drop, for all his care, yet tho' he made me ride Post to Town, to meet the Fool he has pick'd out for me; it shall cost me a fall, if

I don't

I don't marry the Man I have a mind to; I shall see who's the best Politician, my Dad, or I.

Luc. Thy Courage gives fresh Life and Liberty,
To poor *Lucasia*'s tyred restless Soul,
Such pow'r have chearful Friends t'ease our Sorrows.
Oh! my *Lavinia*, may thy Councel prove
Prophetick, I'm going now, in this disguise, to meet my
Dear *Palante*; may no malignant Star
Interpose, to cross our mutual Wishes.
May thy Designs successful prove,
To fix thee ever in *Francisco*'s Arms.

Lav. And make *Palante* yours.

Scene, *The Street.* Sancho *and* Francisco *meeting.*

Fran. Don *Sancho* your Servant; Who thought of seeing you at *Palermo*, I thought you had been at the University of *Salamanca*?

Sancho. I came lately from thence.

Fran. Prithy, what brought you hither?

Sancho. Why, that that brings some Men to the Gallows, a Wench.

Fran. What, I warrant, you have got your Bed-maker with Child, and so are expell'd the College.

Sancho. That's a mistake.

Fran. What, thou art not come hither to take Physick, ha!

Sancho. No, not the Physick you mean; but I am going to enter into a Course, that is, the Course of Matrimony.

Fran. Matrimony, with who, prithy?

Sancho. Why, with Don *Larich*'s Daughter: Do you know her?

Fran. Ha! Is this my Rival? This was a lucky Discovery, (*aside*) know her, ay, very well, Sir. I can assure you she's
very

very handsome, and as Witty as she is Fair; Thou won't visit her in that Dress, sure?

Sancho. To chuse, Sir, 'tis an Emblem of Learning; nay, I design my Man shall carry a load of Books along with me too, that she may see what he is Master of, that is to be Master of her.

Fran. Indeed, my Friend, you'll never succeed upon those Terms.

Tristr. Sir, my Master has such an itch to this foolish Learning, that he bestows more Money yearly upon Books, than would build an Hospital for all the *Courtisans* in *Italy*.

Sancho. No more, or you'll displease me, *Tristram*.

Tristr. I can't help that, Sir— Sir, will you believe me, I have spent two days in sorting Poets from Historians, and as many nights in placing the Divines on their own Chairs, I mean their Shelves, then seperating Philosophers, from those People that kill with a License, cost me a whole day's labour; and tho' my Master says Learning is immortal, I find the Sheets it is contain'd in savors much of mortality.

Sancho. I hope my Books are in good case, *Tristram*?

Tristr. Yes, yes, Sir, in as good case as the Moths have left 'em.

Sancho. Od'so, I had forgot, go get me *Suarez Metaphysicks, Tolet de anima,* and *Granados Commentaries,* on *Primum Secundæ Thomæ Aquinatis.*

Tristr. How the Devil does he do to remember all these Authors hard Names, I dare swear he understands not a Sillable of their Writings— Sir, would not the famous History of *Amidis de Gaul* do as well

Fran Ay, better, better far, Man, harkee *Sancho*, you are not at *Salamanca* now, amongst you Square Caps, but in *Palermo,* come up to see your Mistress the fair *Lavinia,* the glory of the City; go and Court her like a Gentleman, without your Tropes and Figures, or all the Physicks, Metaphysicks, and Metaphors, will streight be made pittiful Martyrs.

Sancho. Martyrs, Sir, why, I thought--- *Fran.*

Fran. Thy self an errant Idiot, thy Brain's more dull than a *Dutch* Burghers Is this a dress fit for a Gentleman to Court his Mistress in? Away, away, the Lady you speak of, I can assure you, is too much a Gallant to be taken with a Band and a square Cap — If you would succeed, you must throw off that Pedant, and assume the Gentleman, learn the toss of the Head, and know the Principles of each man by the cock of his Hatt.

Sancho. How's that, pray?

Fran. Oh! I'll teach you: if you be but willing to improve, I'll warrant you carry the Lady.

Sancho But I am to be married to her as soon as I see her, so my Father told me, and that her Father admired a Scholar above all things.

Fran I'll improve that hint — Aye, as I told you, a Scholar that is read in men, not in Books.

Sancho. In men, what's that? in men! *Tristram*, what does he mean? what man is to be read? In men! I don't understand you; but you'll teach me, you say

Fran Ay, ay, I'll give you a Lesson upon that Subject.

Sancho. Very well: but what shall I do for Cloaths to dress like a Gentleman?

Fran. If you please to step into my Lodgings here, I'll equip you with a Suit of mine till you can have one made, and there I'll teach you a little of the Town breeding, and I warrant you you'll succeed.

Sancho. Come on; faith I long to become thy Scholar.

Fran. And I to make you an Ass. [*Exit.*

Enter Eugeno *and his Man.*

Eug. What can this mean? where e're I come the News is currant of my Death, yet not two days since, I wrote and received Letters from my Father, and here the rumour goes,

I have been dead this fortnight; *I* am resolv'd to know the grounds, if possible. *Pedro*, go get me some disguise, and for your life discover not who *I* am, I'll stay here at this Inn 'till you return. and in the mean time think what method to pursue my Project in. [*Exit.*

Scene changes to the Grove. Lucasia, *Sola*

   Lucasia, Methinks this silent solitary Grove
Should strike a terrour to such Hearts as mine;
But Love has made me bold, the time has been,
In such a place as this, *I* should have fear'd
Each shaking Bough, and started at the Wind,
And trembled at the rushing of the Leaves;
My Fancy would have fram'd a thousand shapes;
But now it seems a Palace.
Delightful as the Poets feign
The *Elizian* Fields: Here do *I* expect
To meet my Love, my faithful, dear *Palante*.
Why does he stay thus long? when last we
Parted, each hour he said wou'd seem a Year,
'Till we were met again, and yet I'm here
Before him; I'll rest a while, for come *I*
Know he will. [*Goes and sits down.*

Enter Palante *and* Clerimont.

  Pal. This, *Clerimont*, this is the happy place,
where *I* shall meet the sum of all my Joys,
And be possest of such a vast Treasure
As wou'd enrich a Monarch to receive;
And thou, my Friend, must give her to my Arms.
  Luc. Tis my *Palante*'s Voice. [*Comes forward.*
  Pal. My Life, my Soul, what here before me? still

Thou

Thou prevent'st me in the race of Love, and
Makeſt all my Endeavours poor, in competition
With thy large favours———
But *I* forget, Deareſt; bid my Friend here welcome,
This is he whom *I* dare truſt, next my own
Heart, with Secrets.

   Luc. *I* muſt admire him that Loves *Palante*;
Friendſhip's a noble Name, 'tis Love refin'd;
'Tis ſomething more than Love, 'tis what *I* wou'd
Shew to my *Palante.*

   Cler. It is indeed a Beauty of the Mind, a Sacred Name,
In which ſo brightly ſhines that Heavenly Love,
That makes th' immortal Beings taſte each others joy;
'Tis the very Cement of Souls. Friendſhip's
A Sacred name, and he who truly knows
The meaning of the Word, is worthy of
Eſtimation
No pains he'll ſpare, no difficulties ſtart,
But hazard all for th' int'reſt of his Friend.

   Pal. Ay! Now methinks I'm Emperour of the World,
With my ineſtimable Wealth about me:
To ſuch a Miſtreſs, ſuch a Friend, what can be
Added more to make me happy?——
Oh! thou darkſome Grove, that won't to be call'd
The Seat of Melancholy, and ſhelter
For the diſcontented Souls! ſure thou'rt wrong'd!
Thou ſeem'ſt to me a place of Solace and Content;
A Paradiſe! that gives me more than Courts
Cou'd ever do: Bleſt be then thy fair Shades,
Let Birds of Muſick always chant it here;
No Croaking Raven, or ill-boding Owl,
Make here their baleful Habitation:
But may'ſt thou be a Grove for Loves fair Queen
To ſport in, for under thy bleſt ſhade two faithful

Lovers

Lovers meet —— Why is my *Lucasia* sad?

Luc. I know not, but *I* long to quit this place,
My Thoughts seem to divine of Treachery,
But whence *I* know not, no Creature's conscious
To our meeting here but *Laura*; I have always
Found her Honest, and yet I would she did not know it.

Pal. 'Tis only Fear assaults thy tender Mind;
But come, my Friend, let's to the Cell adjoyning
To this Grove, and there the Priest
Shall make us one for ever   [*Exeunt.*

Enter Larich *and* Lavinia.

Larich. Come, set your Face in order, for *I* expect young *Sancho* here immediately, he arriv'd in Town last Night, and sent me word but now, he'd be here in an instant.

Lav. But, Sir.

Larich. Sir me no Sirs, for I'm resolv'd you shall be married to Night.

Enter a Servant.

Serv. Sir, here's a Gentleman to wait on you calls himself *Don Sancho*.

Larich. Odso, shew him up; now, you Baggage, you shall see the pink of Learning, one that can travel through the whole World in an Afternoon, and sup in *Palermo* at Night, ha' you shall, you'll be as wise as the *Sibills* in a Months time, with such a Husband, and will bring forth a Race of Politicians that shall set the World together by the Ears, then patch it up again in the supping up of a poach'd Egg.

Enter

Enter Sancho *and* Triſtram.

Larich. Save you, Sir.

Sancho. You don't think me damn'd, Sir, that you beſtow that Salutation upon me?

Larich. By no means, Sir, 'tis only my way of expreſſing a hearty welcome.

Sancho. Sir, your humble Servant: Is this your fair Daughter, Sir?

Larich. Yes, Sir.

Sancho. She's very handſome, Faith.

Larich She's as Heaven made her.

Sancho. Then ſhe ſhou'd be naked; the Taylor ſhou'd have no hand in her— I ſuppoſe you know my Buſineſs, ſhall we be married inſtantly?

Larich. Won't to morrow ſerve, Sir? I wou'd firſt hear a little of your proceedings in the Univerſity; came you from *Salamanco* now, Sir?

Sancho. From *Salamanco*! What do you ſee in my Face, that ſhou'd make you judge me ſuch a Coxcomb?

Larich Your Father writ me word, that his Son that was to marry my Daughter, was a Scholar, wholly given up to Books.

Sancho. My Father was an arrant Aſs for his pains, I ne're read a Book in my life but what I was beat to, and thoſe I forgot as ſoon as I left School: A Scholar! he lies in his Throat that told you ſo.

Lavin. In my Conſcience, Sir, you may believe him; I dare ſwear he never ſaw a Book except the Chronicle Chain'd in his Father's Hall.

Larich. Hold your Tongue, Huſſy; how now?

Sancho Sir, I underſtand a Horſe, a Hawk, or Hound, as well as any man living; nay, I underſtand Men too; I know
now

now that you are an old covetous Hunks, by the sett of your Hatt now; but no matter for that, your Daughter is the better Fortune.

Lavin. The Fool has hit right upon my Father, we shall have rare sport presently.

Sancho. I have studied Men, Sir—— I know each Man's inward Principle by his out-side Habit.

Lavin. Does your profound Knowledge reach to Women too, Sir?

Larich. You will be prating——

Sancho. Look you, Sir, observe the management of my Hatt now—— This is your Bullying Gamester.
[*Three Corners short pinch.*

Larich. What the Devil have we here! s'death this can never be *Don Sancho's* Son?

Lavin. This is indeed the Pink of Learning, Sir—I shall be as wise as the *Sibills* with such a Husband; ha, ha, ha.

Sancho. Your Beaus wear their Hatts [*offering to put it on*] no, hold, thus, Sir; [*clapping it under his Arm*] your conconceited Wit, thus, [*putting it on over the left Eye*] and your travell'd Wit thus [*over the right Eye without a pinch*] your Country Squire, thus, [*putting it behind his Wig.*]

Larich. I wonder how an Ass wears it, I'm sure thou art one; I am amaz'd ! this must be some trick certainly. [*Aside.*

Lavin. What think you now, Sir, shall we get a Race of Politicians? In my Conscience this falls out as well as I could wish. Oh that I could but once see *Francisco.*[*Aside.*

Larich. Huzzy, hold your Tongue, or—— or——
[*Holds up his Cane.*

This may be some of your Contrivance, for ought I know. This is a very great Blockhead; Ounds, I—— I—— I—— have a good mind to add one Fashion more to your Hatt, and knock it down to your Crown.

Sancho. Evermore, Sir, when you see a Man wear his
Hatt

Hat thus [*pulling it down on both sides*] he's a Projector, a Projector, Sir, or a Member of the Society of the Reformation of Manners, [*in another Tone*] What think you of this, Old Gentleman? hah! is not this a greater Knowledge than ever Man attain'd to by Books? hah!

Larich. I admire that my Old Friend, knowing my aversion for these foolish Fopperies, shou'd breed up his Son to 'em, then write me word he had made him a Scholar, purposely because I was a lover of Learning; pray, Sir, was you ever in *Palermo* before?

Sancho. No, Sir; but I like it very well now *I* am in't.

Larich. I must be satisfied that you are Senior *Sancho's* Son, e're *I* shall like you for mine. [*Aside*

Sancho. What think you of a Glass of Champaign, Sir? If you'll go to the Tavern, I'll give you a Bottle of the best the House affords; what say you, Old Dad? ha! and there we will consult about our Marriage.

Larich. If you'll go to the Tavern that joyns to the *Piazza*, I'll wait on you in a quarter of an Hour.

Sancho. Sir, *I* shall wait your pleasure.

Larich. I took the hint to get rid of him, what shall I do to find the truth of this? [*Exeunt.*

Enter a Servant.

Servant. Sir, a Scholar enquires for you.

Larich. A Scholar! admit him immediately.

Enter Francisco *in* Sancho's *Habit.*

Fran. So, *I* watch'd *Sancho* out, now for my Cue. [*Aside.*
If you be the venerable Man to whom this goodly Mansion is impropriated; *I* come to negociate about Authentick Business.

Lav. This rather shou'd be *Don Sancho's* Son ———— his
Words

Words and Habit speak him most learned—— *I* am the Person, pray let me be bold to crave your Name.

Fran. My Appellation, or *pro nomen*, as the Latins term it, is call'd *Jeremie*, but my *Cognomen*, in our Mother Tongue, is call'd *Sancho*.

Lav. Ha! upon my life 'tis *Francisco*; oh, for an opportunity to speak to him: *I* hope to Heaven, my Father won't find out the Cheat. [*Aside.*

Larich Ay, this is he, this is he; what *Don Sancho*'s Son?

Fran. The *Nominals*, the *Thomists*, and all the Sects of Old and Modern School men, do oblige me to pay to that Gentleman filial Duty.

Larich. I am glad to hear it with all my heart, I know the other must be an Impostor, but I'm resolv'd to apprehend and punish him: Sir, you are welcome; *I* guess your Business, my Daughter is yours.

Fran. My Business is about propagation, as the Civil Lawyers do learnedly paraphrase, is of Concomitance, or Cohabitation, or what you please to term it.

Larich. How am *I* blest that this wonderful Scholar shall be matched into my Family—— Daughter, what say you now, here's a Husband for you now, here's a Husband for you

Lavin. Pray Heaven you hold but in the Mind 'till you have made him such. [*Aside.*

Larich. Does he not speak like an Oracle? 'Igad I'll maintain't, he shall put down ten Universities and Inn's of Court in twenty Syllables —— Pray, Sir, speak learnedly to my Girl, for, tho' *I* say it, she has a good Capacity.

Fran. Most rubicund, stilliferous, splendant Lady, the occular faculties, by which the Beams of Love are darted into every Soul, or humane Essence, have convey'd into my Breast the lustre of your Beauty; and *I* can admire no other

ther Object; therefore pardon me, Sir, if I only express my self in Terms Scholastick, and in Metaphors, my Phrase to her. [*Turning to* Larich.

Larich. Learned, Learned, Young Man, how happy am I in thee?

Lavin. Now do I long to see my Father's back turn'd, that he might change his learned non-sense, and talk more Modern, to talk more Wise; you may spare your Rhetorick, Sir, unless you come down to my understanding; but I know just enough of your meaning, to tell you it does not suit with my inclination.

Larich What don't suit with your inclination, ha, forsooth?

Lavin. Marriage, Sir.

Larich. 'Tis false, hussy, you have an inclination, and you shall have an inclination; not an inclination, quoth the baggage: Sir, I say she's yours, come into the next Room, and I'll have the Settlement drawn immediately, and you shall be married to night. Not an inclination! [*Exit.*

ACT III.

SCENE *The Street.*

Enter Eugenio.

Eugen. Thus in Disguise I shall discover all, And find the Cause of my reported Death, Which does so much amaze me.
A Month ago my Father sent me word, that I shou'd hasten my Journey to *Palermo*; and I met the Post upon the Road, that gave me a Letter, wherein he strictly charges me not to come this three Months: No sooner had I enter'd the Town, but I met the rumour of my Death, which still surpris'd me more; but this Letter shall help me to the knowledge of the truth. [*Shews a Letter, goes to the Door and* [*knocks.*

Enter Rosco.

Rosco. Who'd you speak with, Friend?
Eugen. With the Lord *Gravello*, if you please, Sir.

Ros. Marry

Ros. Marry gap, and can't I serve your turn? Nothing but my Lord, good lack! I guess he knows you not; pray what's your business? What's your Name? From whence come you? What do ye want? I believe you are of no such Extraction, that you shou'd be introduc'd to my Lord; let me be judge, whether your affair require his Lordship's Ear, else, Friend, I shall bring you but a scurvy answer; either he's busie, or a-sleep, or gone a-broad, any of these are sufficient for your Quality, I suppose

Eug Thus great Men always are abus'd, because
There's no access, but through such Knaves as thee;
Then I'll return my Message back unto his Son, and bid
him employ a finer Fellow, if he expects that he shou'd see
his Father. [*Going.*

Ros Ha! his Son! stay, Sir, and forgive me; here comes my Lord

Enter Count Gravello, Rosco *goes and whispers him.*

Gra Wou'd you ought with me, Friend?
Eug. If you be the Lord *Gravello.*
Gra. The same.
Eug. I came from *Rome*, my Lord; Laden, I hope, with happy Tidings, and after the sad report I have met with, I dare say, welcome; your Son *Eugenio* lives, and with his Duty, recommends this Letter to your Lordships perusal. [*Gives him a Letter.*

Gra. How! does my Boy live? Oh! I'm overjoy'd, for I thought him Dead. *Rosco* Reward him for his Tidings, Reward him largely, *Rosco.*

Ros. There's

Rof. There's a Piftol for you, eat like an Emperour, d'ye hear, till that be out.

Gra. He Writes me word, that you are a Gentleman fallen to decay, and begs that *I* would take you into my Service: *I* have no place vacant at prefent, but the firft that falls worth your acceptance, fhall be yours, in the mean time Command my Houfe, [*I muft not let him fufpect I knew Eugenio was alive*] the happy News that thou haft brought me, has rais'd me from the Vale of Death; but tell me, Friend, haft thou reveal'd this to any in *Palermo*, but my felf?

Eug. To none. For tho' *I* met the Tragick Story in every Street through which *I* pafs'd, ftill *I* conceal'd the truth, intending your Lordfhips Ear fhould firft receive it.

Gra. Thou haft done exceeding well; *Rofco*, give him a double Reward, a double welcome; *I* have fome private Reafons to my felf that it fhould ftill be kept a fecret, which if thou'rt faithful, thou in time fhalt know.

Eug. Fear not, my Lord, I am no blab; I ever thought a flippery Tongue Mankind's fhame. What can this mean? [*Afide.*

Rof. This is a notable Fellow.

Gra. Rofco, bid him welcome; tell him my Houfe is his, bid him be free.

Rof As long as you have occafion for him —— Sir, I am your moft Obedient, moft Devoted, and thrice Humble Serviteur; Command the Pantry, Cellar, Maids, Chambers, —— for in thefe I rule, and thefe are at your Service, Sir. [*Bowing low.*

Eug. I thank you my Quondam Friend; but a Quiet refidence in my Lord's Houfe, the time I ftay, fatisfies my defires.

Rof. A worthy man, upon my Faith. Oh! my Lord, here comes the Bridegroom, I know by this Fellow's being out of breath.

Enter

Enter a Servant.

Serv. My Lord Count *Pirro* so fine, so brisk, so ugly.
Gra. How, how, Sirrah, ugly?
Serv. So handsome, I mean, Sir; Pox on't, how came my Head to run so of Ugliness?
Rosco. Seeing the Count, I warrant thee, *Jack*.
Gra. Be gone, Varlet, and attend his comeing. [*Exeunt.*
Eugene. Ha! Count *Pirro* the Bridegroom— and, my Life a Secret; I begin to find the Cause. [*Aside.*

Enter Count Pirro.

Pir. I came, my Lord, to claim your Promise, and Receive into my Arms the Beautiful *Lucasia*.
Gra. And I'll acquit my self instantly. Within there— call *Lucasia*.

Enter Laura.

Laura. My Lord.
Grav. My— call your Lady; what does your flurtship do here? *I* want your Mistress— why don't the Wench stir?
Laura. My Lord, I don't know.—
Gra. What don't you know? nay, no grinding between your Teeth, speak out.
Laur. Why then, my Lord, *I* don't know where she is.
Gra. 'Tis false, 'tis impossible; when went she out? and whither? Speak ye confederate Mischief; how long ago, I say? Confess, or I'll have you rack'd.
Lau. She would not take me with her to prevent suspicion; and now all must out, for my Limbs will never bear stretching, that's certain. [*Aside.*
Gra. What

Gra. What are you inventing a Lye? —— don't stand muttering your Devil's *Pater noster* there, but speak quickly —— or —— [*Draws his Sword.*

Lau. Oh hold, it was, my Lord, my Lord, a, a, a ——

Gra. What was it? speak.

Lau. It was a great while ago my Lord.

Gra. Ha, speak to the purpose, or thou dy'st.

Lau. No, no, no, my Lord, it was —— it was just now; what shall I say to save my unhappy Mistress? [*Aside.*

Pirro. You terrifie the Creature so, that we shall never learn the truth, my Lord, don't tremble so sweetheart, but tell when went your Lady out, and whither?

Gra. Away, my Lord, my Sword shall fetch the Secret forth; Huzzy, speak, or by this Hand, this Minute is thy last. [*Holds his Sword to her Breast.*

Lau. Oh, hold Sir, and I will tell you all; I do confess.

Gra. What?

Lau. It must out; that my Lady's fled to meet *Palante* in the Eastern Grove, and *I* believe, by this, they are married.

Gra. Fly, and escape my Fury, thou more than Devil. [*Straps her with his Sword, she shrieks and runs off.*
Now, my Lord of *Pirro*, you that so kindly came this day to comfort me, how shall I look you in the Face? or what reparation can I make you, if my Daughter's lost? Within there! raise the House, take Officers immediately, I charge you; fly to the Eastern Grove, and seize my Daughter and all that you find with her: we'll have revenge, my Lord, at least.

Pirro. There's yet a Pleasure left in that, and I'm resolv'd my Arm shall give him Death; let's to the Grove, my Lord.

Rosco. Do you consider, my Lord, the danger of your rash Attempt, the Law will do you right; 'tis present Death in *Sicily*, to steal an Heiress without her Friends consent; first secure him, and his Life's yours: *Eug.* 'Tis

Eug. 'Tis as I suppose; oh Treachery! [*Aside.*

Gra. Rosco, thou art an Oracle, that way the Revenge is more secure and certain. I'll after 'em, and see the Traytor brought to condign punishment. [*Exit with* Rosco.

Pirro. I'll to the Governour, and prepare him for the Judgment, my Interest there will surely sign his Death
[*Going.*

Eug. Am I alive? do I breath? can I have a humane Soul, and suffer this injustice to proceed? Poor *Palante,* must thou die, because Fortune has not blest thee with her Favours? No, something I will do to save thee; and yet, if possible, not discover who I am. My Lord——
[*Pulls Count* Pirro *by the Sleeve as he goes out.*

Pirro. What art thou?

Eug. A poor Poet, my Lord, little beholden to Fortune.

Pirro None of thy Profession are, take up some more thriving Occupation; turn Pimp, Sollicitor, Gamester, any thing will do better than rhiming; there's something for thee, I'm in haste now.

Eug. My Lord, I thank you for your Charity, and your good Advice; but I have some for you too.

Pirro For me! what is't?

Eug I understand, my Lord, that you are to marry my Lord *Gravello*'s Daughter.

Pirro. Yes, an Heiress——

Eug. No Heiress, my Lord, her Brother is alive.

Pirro. The Fellow's mad——

Eug. What I say is certain truth; and to my Knowledge, his Father gives out the report of his Death only as a Bait for you.

Pirro. Ha! where is he?

Eug. In this Town conceal'd 'till your Marriage be over; know I hate this Family, and that makes me discover it.

Pirro. Does he hate the Family? then perhaps he has only

ly forg'd this Lye to hinder *Lucasia* from marrying into mine; I'll try him farther [*Aside.*
Art thou sure he is alive?

Eug. As sure as that I live my self; my Lord, I saw him not two Hours ago, I wish he was not, for your Lordships sake: I am his Domestick, and come now to learn Intelligence, I loath my Servitude, detest the proud Family, and shou'd rejoyce to see 'em ruin'd.

Pirro. From whence proceeds thy hate? the World reports *Engenio* a Man of Honour, Honesty and Courage.

Eug. That part of the World that thinks him such, sees thro' the wrong end of the Prospective; his Honour's but pretence, his Honesty Hypocrisie, and his Courage lewdness, he ravisht a Sister of mine at *Rome*, for which I never can forgive him.

Pirro. This Fellow, I find is ripe for Mischief; and if I durst trust him, wou'd, for a large Reward, remove *Eugenio*, and make *Lucasia* indeed an Heiress, and 'twere but just, since Count *Gravillo* did design to wrong me of his Estate, why shou'd not I rob him of his Son? where could be the danger of this Act? I can't fore-see any, for he has already given it out he's dead, and therefore dares not search into the matter; but is it safe to trust this Stranger, he may betray my purpose, or not do it; yet 'tis reasonable to think the contrary, for he hates him for his Sister's Rape, and therefore would be glad to meet occasion to revenge it, especially when usher'd in by a great *sum:* I'm resolv'd to break it to him. [*Aside.*] What is your Name, Friend?

Eug. Irus, my Lord.

Pirro. Your Name as well as Habit speak you poor.

Eug. I'm poor enough, my Lord.

Pirro. Very poor?

Eug. Very poor, my Lord.

Pirro. Would you not gladly mend your Fortunes.

Eug. I

Eug. I wish your Lordship wou'd shew me the way.

Pirro. What think you now of taking revenge for your Sister's Rape, ha?

Eug. Alas! my Lord, that I wou'd have done long ago, but want prevented my escape.

Pirro. Say'st thou so? my Friend: well, poison this *Eugenio*, and thou shalt not want; for thy Reward, a thousand Crowns are thine.

Eug. Think it done, my Lord, nor will I receive my hire till I have brought you a certain proof *Eugenio* is no more; all I ask is but your Hand to the Agreement, my Lord, that I may be sure of my Reward.

Pirro. I'll give it thee —— We must be safe, for his Father will be asham'd to Prosecute, after his reported Death. I must confess I lov'd *Lucasia* as an Heiress, but was she ten times as fair, I would not marry her without the Dowry, therefore make sure my Fortune by thy Master's Death.

Eug. He dies this Night.

Pirro. Follow me, and I'll sign the Contract, then to the Governours. [*Exit.*

Scene changes to the Grove. Palante, Lucasia, *and* Clerimont.

Pal. 'Tis done, 'tis done, the Sacred Knot is ty'd,
And Bright *Lucasia* is for ever mine.
I ne're 'till now did taste the sweets of life;
Or the transporting extasie of Joy.
Burst not ye feeble Ministers of Nature,
With the vast excess of swelling Pleasure.
Oh! my Friend, what shall I say to thee?

Cler. This is no time for talk, or transports, make use of
My fortune, and fly 'till their pursuit is over.

Pal. Oh! *Clerimont*, I'm Bankrupt every way,
Both to thee, and to my Fair *Lucasia*.
Still thou art sad, my Love.

F

Luc.

Luc. My sadness does proceed from fear for thee,
Take your Friend's Counsel, let us fly this place.
Hark! What noise is that? ah me, we're lost

Enter Gravello, Eugenio, Rosco, *and Officers.*

Gra. Fall on, Officers, there they are
Cler. Thieves
Pal. Villains!
Gra Thou art thy self the Thief and Villain too,
Give me my Daughter, thou Ranter.
Pal. First take my Life.
Gra. Fall on, I say, down with 'em if they resist
Luc. Oh! we are undone, wicked, wicked *Laura*
Pal Come on, Slaves   [*They Fight, but are disarm'd by*
Cler. We shall not surrender tamely.   [*the multitude.*
Gra. So, keep 'em fast, we'll have 'em faster shortly.
For you, Minion, *I* shall secure you from a second scape.
Luc. Yet do but hear me, Father
Gra. Call me not Father, thou disobedient wretch,
Thou Vagabond, thou art no Child of mine,
My Daughter was bred up to Virtue
Luc. For you my Mother wou'd have done as much:
If need had so required;
Think not that my mind e're stray'd from Virtue;
Oh! listen to the Voice of Prayer, and Crown
It with rich mercy.
Gra Off, Strumpet, Officers away with the Criminals,
They both shall dye
Pal. Now *I* must speak, oh spare my Friend, for he
Is innocent.
Cler If thou must die, *Palante*, *I* have no
Other wish, but to suffer with thee
Gra. That wish assure thy self thou shalt obtain.
                                              Luc. Oh!

Luc. Oh stay blood-thirsty men, stay and hear me
But a Word, and that shall be my final resolution.
If thou, my cruel Father, wilt not hear,
But dost proceed to spill the blood of him
In whom my life subsists, remember, Sir,
I am your Daughter, once you did love me,
Oh! tell me then, what fault can be so great
To make a Father Murtherer of his Child?
For so you are in taking his dear life;
Do not think that I will stay behind him.
No, whilst there's Asps, and Knives, and burning Coals;
No *Roman* Dame's Example shall outgo
My love.

   Pal. Oh! my *Lucasia*, thou hast touch'd my Soul!
Barely but to imagine thou must die,
Will make me restless in my silent Grave.
Is not my Death sufficient, barbarous Man?
But must *Lucasia*'s woe be added too?
Dry up those Tears my Wife, my lovely Bride,
Or thou wilt make me truly miserable.
Preserve thy Life, that I may after Death,
In thee my better part survive.
For thee and for my Friend my only Prayers shall be,
If you both live, *Palante* dies with pleasure.

   Gra. Away with 'em, and let the Law decide it.

   Luc. I too alike am Guilty;
Oh let me share the punishment with them,
Thou shalt not go alone, take me with thee;
Here are my willing hands, quick bind 'em fast, [*Runs and*
Else here I'll hold 'till my last breath expires. [*clasps* Palante.

   Gra. Ungracious Viper, let go the Traytor.

   Luc. What to dye? Oh, never!

   Pal. Had I a hundred lives, the venture had
Been small for such a Prize.

A Face not half so fair as thine has arm'd
Whole Nations in the Field for Battel ripe
And brought a thousand Sail to *Tenedos*,
To sack lamented *Troy*, and shou'd *I* fear
To hazard one poor life for thee, my fair?
A life that had been lost, without thy love,
For thou'rt both Life and Soul to thy *Palante*.

  Luc. I'll clasp him like the last remains of life, [*Holds him.*
And struggle still with never dying love

  Gra Then thus I dash thee from him, thou stranger
                    [*Pushes her, and falls down.*
To my blood, there lye and grovel on the Earth, and thank the
Powers I do not kill thee; away to Justice with the Traytors.

  Pal If there be a torment beyond this sight,
Then lead me to it, that I may taste all
The variety of misery, and
Grow compleatly wretched
Oh, Inhumane cruelty!
Slaves give me way, that swift as Lightning,
I may dash him dead that wrong'd *Lucasia*
You spiteful Powers show'r all your Curses down,
Augment the weight, and sink me all at once.

  Gra. Away with the Traytor.

  Pal. Oh! Let me first embrace my Love, my Wife.

  Gra. By Hell, he shall not

  Pal. So when a Ship by adverse Winds is tost,
And all the hopes to gain the Port is lost,
The trembling Mariners to Heaven cry,
And all in vain, for no relief is nigh
Around fierce terrors strike their aking sight;
So I when shut from that all charming light,
Like them must plunge in everlasting night. [*Ex. Forc'd off.*

  Gra. I'll to the Governour, and urge my injur'd Suit. *Rosco*
and *Irus*, Guard that wretched Woman; take care that she
neither sends nor receives a Message   [*Ex.*   *Ros.*

Rosco. Yes, my Lord.

Eug. My very Heart bleeds to see two such faithful Lovers parted; methinks my Lord's too cruel in this action.

Ros Ay, ay, Friend: but we are to Obey, not to dispute his Will.

Eug I can scarce forbear revealing my self, but I will reserve it for a fitter Hour, her grief's so great, I fear it has depriv'd her of her Senses; look up, Madam.

Luc. Where's my *Palante*, gone to death? Oh Heav'n!
When shall I be mad indeed? what are you,
Officers of Justice? I'm ready, Sir.

Eug. No, Madam, I am one my Lord your Father left to attend you

Luc Attend me! alas, I need no Attendance.

Eug. Do not reject my service.

Luc All service comes too late to miserable me;
My Fortune's desperate grown.

Eug. Believe me, Madam, I have a feeling Woe;
A greater your own Brother could not have:
Think not I'm subborn'd to do you wrong,
By all the Powers I'm your trusty Friend,
Command me any thing, and try my Faith.

Rosco. This is a rare spoken Fellow; I can't put in a word.

Luc. Oh! 'tis most prodigious,
Cou'd I lose pity in a Father's Breast,
And find it in a Stranger's? I shall not
Live to thank you, Sir, but my best Prayers go
With you.

Eug. 'Tis not for Thanks, nor for Reward I look,
But the sacred Love I bear to Virtue,
makes me offer this.

Luc. Surely this poor Man is nobly bred, howe're
His Habit speaks him. [*Aside.*

All

All Physick comes too late to my sick Mind,
Since there's no hopes of my *Palante*'s Life.

Eug. Unless the Governour will please to pardon him;
'twas good that he were mov'd.

Rosco. Be not so forward, Friend, I say; in my Conscience this Fellow will betray *Eugenio* lives.

Eug Peace, Fool.

Ros You are something free, methinks.

Luc. Who shall dare to make that Supplication?
My Father and the Count of *Pirro* rules,
Yet I wou'd venture, if I knew which way

Eug. So meritorious is the Act, that I wou'd stand the Test in giving you the liberty to sue.

Rosco How, Sir?

Eug. Peace, Muckworm, or my Sword shall stop thy Breath for ever

Rosco A desperate Fellow this, I dare not contradict him.

Luc. A thousand Blessings on you for your care.
Yes, I will go, grant it ye Powers above,
If you had e're regard to injur'd Love:
Teach me such words as may his pity move,
Let it pierce deep into his stony Heart,
In all my Sufferings make him feel a part
Oh make him feel the pangs of sharp Despair,
That he may know what wretched Lovers bear.
My Sighs and Tears shall with Intreaties joyn,
That he would save *Palante*'s Life, or sentence mine:
But if relentless to My Prayers he be,
And he must fall, then welcome Destiny.
Fate does our Lives so close together twine,
Who cuts the Thread of his, unravels mine. [*Exeunt.*

Scene

SCENE, *the Governour's House.*

Enter the Governour *and Count* Pirro.

Gov. Welcome, my dearest Nephew, you are grown a Stranger to the Court of late, tho' you know my aged Sight receives no joy without you; but I can forgive you since Love is the Cause: I hear you have the Lord *Gravello*'s Consent to marry the fair *Lucasia*

Pirro. I had, my Lord, but am unjustly robb'd Of that fair Prize you mention; my promis'd Bride is stol'n by *Palante,* Lord *Euphenes*'s Foster-Son, a Man far unworthy of *Lucasia*'s Love; her Father's with Officers are gone to apprehend 'em ——
And bring 'em here before you to receive their doom· Oh, Uncle, if ever you had a kindness for me; if the being ally'd to you by Blood, or ought *I* have done, or can hereafter do, let me intreat you to give the Law its utmost Course· Young *Clarimont* too assisted in the Rape.

Gov. Fear not, Nephew, the Law shall have its Course, and they shall surely die.

Enter Euphenes *and Count* Gravello *at several Doors*

Euph. My Lord, the Governour, *I* am come begging to you, for *Palante* my Foster-Son, whom, Childless, I adopted for my own; for him *I* plead.

Gov. What is his Offence?

Euph. No heinous Crime, my Lord, no treasonable Plot against your Person or the State, for then these aged Cheeks wou'd blush to ask Pardon.

No

No crying Murther ſtains his Hands, his Fault is only Love Unfortunately he has married the Daughter and Heireſs to that proud Lord that follows, and ſeeks the laſt extremity.

Gra. I ſeek no more than what the Law will give; I am abus'd, my Lord, my Daughter is ſtoll'n, the only Comfort of my Age; Juſtice, my Lord, 'tis Juſtice that I ask.

Per. To his juſt ſuit I bend my knees —— be not biaſs'd by ought but Juſtice.——

Eug. Thou ſpeakeſt like an Enemy, call it Revenge —— not Juſtice —— My Lord.——

Gov. I'll hear no more, be ſilent, if the Law will ſave him, he ſh— live, if not, he dies; yes, my Lord, you ſhall have Juſtice —— [*Exeunt*

SCENE *changes to Gravello's Houſe*

Enter Larich, Franciſco, *and* Lavinia.

Larich Body, oh me! here's mad work abroad my Niece is ſtoll'n; I'm reſolv'd to make ſure of you, the Prieſt ſhall joyn you inſtantly.

Fran. Haſte, Sir, to conſummate our Joy.
I'll call the Muſes from their ſacred Hill,
To emulate your Daughter's Beauty,
And I'll, my ſelf, in lofty Numbers ſing my own Epithalamium

Larich Firſt, I'll puniſh that Impoſter —— Here, bring in the Priſoner.

Lavin. Oh! I fear we are undone, *Franciſco*.

Fran. Pray, Father, delay not my exorbitant Deſires.

Larich But for a Moment, learn'd Son,
And thy exorbitant Deſires ſhall be ſatisfi'd

Enter

San. Fackings *Tristram*, he's woundy out of humour, I have fob'd him now faith, he, he, he.

Larich. Sir, I desire your Scholastick breeding wou'd quit my temporal habitation to *Franscisco*, least I commit you to a closer place, and thank this Gentleman for your liberty, 'tis because he has some small acquaintance with you, that I don't proceed in a rougher manner.

Fran. I am defenceless now, but I shall find a time. (*exit.*

Larich. To be hang'd I hope, come Mrs. I suppose you had a hand in this wise Plot, I'll prevent your Stratagems, I'll noose and fetter you in the Chains of Wedlock, then if you Plot, let *Sancho* look to't.

For when they are wedd the Father's care is done.

Trist. And the poor doting Husband's just begun.

The end of the Third Act.

ACT. IV.

SCENE the Governour's House.
The Governour in a Chair reading.

Gov. I Have been searching over all our *Sicilian* Laws, and know they cannot find one clause to save *Palante.* (*Enter a Servant.*)

Serv. A Lady without, my Lord will not be denied your Presence.

Gov. Admit her.

Enter Lucasia.

Luc. Pardon me, Sir, for pressing thus rudely
On your privacy, I know 'tis boldness.
But I hope the hour's propitious to me,
Finding you alone, and free from business,
I promise my self I shall be heard with patience.

Gov. Were the business of the world at stake, such
Beauty would claim a hearing, Speak Madam.

Luc. Thus

Euc. Thus Low I beg for poor *Palante*'s Life.
Gov. Ha!
Luc. Oh, Sir,
If ever pitty touch'd your Gen'rous breast.
If ever Virgins Tears had power to move,
Or if you ever lov'd and felt the pangs
That other Lovers do, pity Great, Sir,
Pity and Pardon two unhappy Lovers,

Gov. Your life is not in question, Madam,

Luc. If *Palante* dies, I cannot live, for we
Have but one heart, and can have but one fate.

Gov. What I can do, I will to save him, but Law must have its course, rise Madam.

Luc. Never till———
The gracious word of pardon raises me,
There's pitty in your Eye, oh! shew it, Sir!
And say that he shall live, 'tis but a word,
But oh, as welcome as the breath of Life,
Why will you part two hearts that Heav'n has joyn'd?
He is my Husband, Sir, and I his wedded Wife.

Gov. That can plead no excuse, for 'tis your Crime, but if I shou'd incline to pitty you, what wou'd you return? what wou'd you do to purchase the life of him you hold so dear?

Luc. You cannot think the thing I wou'd not do.
Speak, Sir, and lay it but in my power,
And even beyond my power, I will attempt.

Gov. You wou'd be thankful then shou'd I pardon him?

Luc. If I were ever thankful unto Heav'n
For all that I call mine, my health and being,
Cou'd I then be unthankful unto you,
For a gift I value more than those?
Without which all other blessings will be tasteless.

Gov. Those

Gov. Those that are thankful study to requite, wou'd you do so?

Luc. As far as I am capable I will,
Tho' I can ne're make ample satisfaction,
All my Services to you are Duty,
But to those Pow'rs above that can requite
That from their wastless Treasure daily heap
Rewards more out of Grace than Merit on
Us Mortals,
To those I'll pray that they wou'd give you, Sir,
More Blessings, than I have skill to ask.

Gov. There rises one way and but one to save him.

Luc. Oh! name it Sir, that ─────
Swift as the Arrow from the Archers hand
My trembling Feet may fly to save him,
Oh! you have rais'd me from the gulph of Grief
To that blest comfortable Region, Hope,
My Sences all dance in the cirque of Joy.
My ravish't Heart leaps up to hear your Words.
And seems as 'twou'd come forth to thank you.
Say, how, how shall I save him?

Gov. Marry my Nephew *Pirro* and *Palante* lives.

Luc. Oh! unexpected turn of rigid Fate,
Cruel, Sir, far more cruel than my Father.
Why did you raise me to a height of Joy?
To sink me in a moment down again,
In what a sad Delemma stands my Choice,
Either to Wed the Man my Soul most loaths,
Or see him die for whom alone I live,
To break my sacred Vows to Heav'n and him,
To save a Life which he would scorn to take
On terms like those, name any thing but that,
You are more just than to enforce my Will,
Why should I marry one I cannot Love,

And

And sure I am I cannot Love Count *Pirro*,
Love him! no, I shou'd detest and loath him
The cause that made him mine, wou'd hourly add
Fresh matter for my hate.

 Gov. You have your choice, I swear by Heaven never to pardon him, but upon these conditions.

 Luc. Oh! I am miserable.

 Gov. 'Tis your own fault, come consider Madam, *Palante* will thank you for his Life, and if you let him die, you are the Tyrant.

 Luc. I shou'd be such if I should save him thus,
Since you have swore not to save him upon
Other terms, I'll shew a duteous cruelty
And rather follow him in Death than so
To buy his Life, no, I despise the price.
Why do I breath my Woes, or beg for mercy here,
Or hope to find plain Honesty in Courts?
No, their Ears are always stop'd against Justice,
Avarice and Pride supplies the place of Pity.
 So may just Heav'n when you for mercy sue,
 As you have pitied me so pardon you. (*Exeunt severally.*

SCENE Count Gravello's-House.

Enter Larich, Lavinia, Sancho *and* Tristam.

 San. Is the Priest ready *Tristram*?

 Tris. Yes, yes, Sir, a Preist and a Lawyer are always in readiness, their Tongues are the chief Instrument belongs to their

their Trade, with which they commonly do more mischief than all the Chyrurgeons in the Kingdom can heal, he waits in the next Room, Sir, if you can get the Lady in the mind.

Larich. You are witty Sirrah, but no more of your jests, do ye hear, leaft I make you experience, there's something else can do mischief besides their Tongues, come Mistress what you are in the dumps now, are you? dry up your Eyes and go about it cheerfully, or I'll turn you out of doors, I assure you.

Lavin. Good, Sir, consider.

Larich. Consider! no I won't consider, nor shall you consider upon ought but what I'de have you.

Lavin. Sir, do you persfwade him (*to Sancho*), think how unhappy I shall make you.

San. Make me happy first, and then I'll do any thing you'd have me.

Trif. The wisest bargain I ever heard my Master make.

Lavin. What wou'd you do, Sir, with me that cannot love you? Alas I was engaged long before I saw you, you may be happier far elsewhere, go court some Nymph whose Heart's intirely free, such only can be worthy of your love.

San. For my part I don't know what to say.

Larich. Zdeath she'll persfwade him by and by to quit his pretences to her,——come, come, come Mistress no more of your Cant. (*Pulls her by the Arm.*) It shall avail you nothing I'll promise you.

Lavin. Good, Sir, hold a little, *Don Sancho* seems disposed to hear Reason.

San. Why ay truly, for my part methinks it is a pitty to vex the Lady so.

Lavin. Besides, Sir, 'tis for his sake I do it, to make him easie and to prevent his eternal shame and torture.

San. Poor Fool, how hard it is, ay, ay, I know 'tis for my sake, pray, Sir, hear her——pray do for my sake as she says.

Larich.

Larich. Pooh Fool.

Sancho. Shall she say more for my sake, than you'll hear Father that is to be.

Larich. Well huzzy, consider what you say, for if it ben't to the purpose, as I'm sure it won't —— look to't?

Lavin. Before your hasty rashness betrays me to eternal woe, revoke your harsh commands.

Larich. Ay, I knew that would follow, and this is all you have to say Mistress, ha? come, come woe, I'll woe you.

Lavin. Something I have to speak, but know not in what words to dress my thoughts fit for me to speak, or you to hear, oh spare the poor remains of my already too much violated Modesty, — Heav'n can I do this, but there is no other way. *(aside.*

Larich. How? how? how's that? Modesty! why what a duce is the matter with your Modesty, ha?

Lavin. Oh! Sir, force me not to wrong a Man whose Father I have so often heard you say, you lov'd, think what sure disgrace will follow, how will it reflect upon your Name and Family, when I shall be found no Virgin.

Larich. Ha! no Virgin? take heed Minnion that you stain not the Honour of my House, for if you do, I swear by the best Blood in *Sicily,* my Sword shall do me Justice.

Lavin. Now help me courage, and forgive me Heaven my resolutions, Death or my *Francisco.* *(aside.*

I throw my self beneath your feet, thus prostrate beg for mercy, that I have deserved Death my guilty blushes own, the mighty secret hangs upon my tongue, but shame refuses utterance to my words.

Larich. I'm all of a cold Sweat, Heav'ns! how I dread the end of her discourse.

Sancho. Pray Father let her rise, or I shall weep too.

H   *Tris.* Nay

Trif. Nay, I'll say that for my Master, he's as tractable as a Monkey, and generally does what he sees other people do (*aside.*

Lavin. Oh! let it still remain unknown, and rather banish me, confine me to some horrid Desart, there to live on Rots and withered Grafs, and with the falling Dew, still quench my thirst, and lastly to some savage Monster be a Prey, e're I divulge my shame.

San. I can hold no longer. (*Cries aloud.*

Larich. On, for I'll hear it all, tho thou shalt live no longer than thou hast told thy tale.

Lavin. Sure ne're before was Maid thus wretched, Oh *Francisco!* I gave thee here the greatest proof of Love that ever Woman gave——if it must out, then with it take my life, but Oh! spare the innocent Babe.

Larich. Ha! the Babe?

Lavin. Oh! I am with Child.

Larich. Then die both, and both be damn'd. (*Offers to stab her, but is prevented by* Sancho *and* Tristram.

Sanc. Oh, Lord, Sir, for Heav'ns sake, Sir, are you mad, help *Tristram*.

Larich. Zdeath a Whore! Oh thou scandal of my Blood.

San. Egad I'm resolv'd to own the Child, and Bully this old fellow a little now————a Whore, Sir! who dares call my Wife a Whore? the Child is mine, Sir, let me see who has any thing to say to't.

Larich. Away don't trifle with me, I shall not give you credit.

San. What care I whether you do or no, I say again the Child is mine, Madam, dry your Eyes, I like you ne're the worse, and the World will like me the better for't, will bring into reputation.

Lavin.

Lavin. Oh Heavens! what will come on me now, Oh! fly me, Sir, as you wou'd shun Contagion, cou'd you receive into your Arms a wretch polluted by another.

San. Pish, shaw, pish, shaw, 'tis the least thing in a thousand, thou saidst thou didst it for my sake just now, and sure I shou'd return the kindness, Ingratitude is worse than the Sin of Witchcraft.

Larich. Oh! the audacious Strumpet give me way, that I may punish the offence as it deserves.   (*Francisco within.*

Fran. Slaves give me way, he dies that barrs my entrance.

Lavin. Ha! 'tis my *Francisco's* Voice ———— Oh! blest Minute.

Larich. Ha! what noise is that?   (*Help, Murder, cryed within.*

San. How Murder within and Murder without too, this is a barbarous House, I wish I was safe out on't. *Tristram* stand by thy Master.

Trif. Oh, Sir, I had rather run with you, for I hate Murther in cool Blood.

Enter Francisco *with his Sword drawn.*

Larich. Help within there, Murther, you wont Murther me Sirrah, ha? (*Enter 3 or 4 Servants*). run for the Corrigidore, I shall be Murther'd in my own House.

Fran. No, Sir, this Sword can never hurt the Father of *Lavinia*, nor will my arm guide it to any act unjust, nor is it drawn for ought but to defend my Wife.

Larich. Impudent Rascal, can'st thou look me in the face, and know how thou has injur'd me, thou hast dishonour'd my Daughter.

Sanc. Sir, I say no Man has dishonour'd her but my self, and I wonder you shou'd tax this honest Gentleman with it.

Fran. Ha!

Fran. Ha, Villain! re-call what you have said, or by Heaven 'tis thy laſt, 'tis ſafer playing with a Lyon, than with *Lavinia*'s Fame. (*Holding his Sword at his teeth.*

Sanc. Lavinia's Fame, what Fame, what makes you ſo Cholerick, I thought I ſhou'd do the Lady a kindneſs in it.

Triſt. Many a Man wou'd have been glad to have got rid of it ſo.

Lavin. Humour my Father in what he ſays, for 'twas my laſt Stratagem to defer my Marriage (*aſide to* Franciſco.

Larich. Lavinia's Fame! No Monſter, thou haſt rob'd, rob'd her of her Fame.

Fran. The wrong my Love has done your fair Daughter, 'tis now two late to wiſh undone again, but if you pleaſe it may be clos'd up yet without diſhonour, I will Marry her.

Larich. Marry her! ſhe'll have a mighty bargain of that, Marry a Beggar, what Joynture can'ſt thou make her?

Fran. I am poor, I muſt confeſs in regard of your large Wealth, but I ſwear by all things that can bind, 'twas not your Wealth, was the foundation of true built Love, it was her ſingle uncompounded ſelf, her ſelf without addition that I lov'd, which ſhall ever in my heart out-weigh all other Women's Fortunes with themſelves, and were I great, great as I cou'd wiſh my ſelf for her advancement, no ſuch barr as fortunes inequality ſhou'd ſtand betwixt our Loves.

Larich. Say you ſo, Sir, why then take her——there hang, drown'd or ſtave together, I care not which, but never come within my doors more. (*Throws her to him.*
(*Exit* Larich

San. Hy

Sanc. Hy day, what have I loft my Miftrefs then, why what muft I fay to my Father, *Triftram*, who'll run ftark mad without hopes of a Grandfon.

Trift. Oh, Sir, if this Gentleman had not put in his claim, here had been one ready to his hands.

Sanc. Ah pox on't, 'tis dam'd unlucky, but come let's to the Tavern and drink away Sorrow.   (*Exeunt.*

Fran. Come my fair *Lavinia*, and find a Father in thy Husbands arms, oh thou charming Excellence, thou something better fure than ever Woman was, the machlefs proof that thou haft given of thy Love fhall be recorded to Pofterity——

Lavin. It is a matchlefs one indeed and I ftrugled long er'e I cou'd bring my felf to own a deed fo diftant from my heart, but it has ferv'd my purpofe, and I glory in it now, but my Fathers laft words methinks chills my blood, how fhall you like the yoak without lineing think you ha!

Fran. Don't wrong my love *Lavinia*, or think that I can want any thing when poffeft of thee,

Love fhall make up what Fortune does deny,
And love alone fhall all our wants fupply.   (*Exeunt.*

The

The SCENE *changes to the Street, Count* Pirro *and Lord* Gravillo.

Grav. Now my Lord she's your's again, *Palante* dies.

Count Pir. So noble were the carriage of the youths that I could almost pitty their hard Sentence

Grav. I admire *Palante's* constancy, he seem'd regardless when the Jury pronounc'd his Sentence, as if he feared not death, but when his friends came on, I observ'd the Tears to fall.

C. Pirro. He begg'd very hard to save his Friend.——

Grav. And his Friend as eagerly to die with him, truly I think *Clerimont's* crime did not deserve death, but our *Sicilian* Laws dooms all to death that have but the least hand in stealing of an Heiress, but see the Lord *Euphenes*, he sticked hard to save his Foster Son, let's avoid him, for I know he'll raile. (*Exit.*

Enter Lord Euphenes.

Euph. Unhappy poor *Palante*, the Law has cast thee in spight of all that I cou'd do to save thee, I'de give my whole Estate to resc e thee from Death: In thee me thought my lost *Lisander* liv'd, and in loosing thee I'm childless now indeed. I lov'd thee like my own Son, I rescu'd the from Pyrates, by which my child was lost.

Enter

Enter Alphonso.

Alphon. Thus once again from twenty years Exile.
(Tost by the storms of fortune to and fro)
Has gracious Heav'n given me leave to tread
My native earth of *Sicily*, and draw
That air that fed me in my Infancy.

Euph. Ha! either my eyes deceive me or 'tis my good old friend *Alphonso*.

Alph. My Lord *Euphenes* ?

Euphen. *Alphonso*, wellcome to *Sicily*, I thought thee dead with my unhappy Son, or what was worse in Slavery, where no Intelligence cou'd find thee, for I have us'd my utmost diligence.

Alph. In part you have guess'd aright, for I have been twenty teadious years in gauling Slavery, for when the *Argives* surprized the Fort, they hurried me on board, and because I made a brave resistance, they ne're wou'd give me leave to offer at my Ransome, so violent was their hate, but now worn-out with age, unfiting for their labour, they turn'd me home, an useless drone, your Son they put on Board another Ship, and by some I heard it rumord, he being wondrous fair, that they design'd to breed him for the Sultan's use, but some years after I heard he was retaken on this Coast.

Euph. Ha !

Alph. I conceal'd his name, least the many Conquests you have gain'd against them shou'd have wing'd their revenge, and made 'em kill the lovely Child, I call'd him *Palante*, have you ever heard of such a one ?

Euph. Oh

Euph. Oh all ye immortal Powers, the very same, I took, and is *Palante* then *Lysander*, and have I found thee once to loose thee ever?

Alph. Ha! what means all this?

Euph. 'Twas nature then that work'd my Soul, and I by inst.nct lov'd him. Oh my *Alphonso*, this discovery comes too late, and instead of bringing Comfort to my age, thou hast plung'd me down in deep dispair.

Alph. Alas, my Lord, how have I err'd? pray explain your self.

Euph. Oh *Alphonso*! the youth thou speak'st of I retook from *Argive* Pyrats, I bred him, and tho not sencible who he was, I lov'd him tenderly: he is this very day condemn'd for stealing of an Heiress, now judge if my grief falls not with weight upon me.

Alph. Unfortunate mischance, is there no way to save him?

Euph. None I fear, but yet I'll try all means, if my long service to my Country, my Winter Camps, and summer heats, and all my stormy fate at Sea can plead, I will expand my deeds as *Rome*'s Consuls did of old, make bare my breast, and shew my 'scar'd Bosome to move and raise their Pitty.

I that ne're mention'd ought my arm has done,
Will now, urge all to save my darling Son. (Exeunt.

ACT.

ACT V.
SCENE a PRISON.

Palante and Clerimont *come forward.*

Palan. OH! *Clerimont*, I Swear by my malignant Stars,
Death brings no Terrors with it but for thee;
The thoughts of thine, and that I have Involv'd
In my sad Fate, my best and only Friend,
Sits heavy on my Soul, and gives me double Death:
My Father's Tears, whom now too late I know,
Pierce not my Breast with half this killing Grief,
This gnaws me worse than my *Lucasia*'s loss;
And, like a *Vulture*, preys upon my Heart.
I was Rewarded, call'd *Lucasia* mine:
For such a Treasure who wou'd refuse to dye?
But thou art it Condemn'd for only aiding me.
I am the Cause of thy sad Fate my Friend;
Hurri'd by me to an untimely Grave:
Thou fal'dst for him thou ever hast oblig'd.

Cler. No more *Palante*——
Why dost thou call me by the Name of Friend?
Yet think I cou'd descend from Friendships Rules.
For so I must shou'd I repine at Death,
Or fear to Suffer with so brave a Man.

To dye is nothing to a Man resolv'd:
Why shou'd we wish to hold this mortal frame,
By Nature subject to such various ills,
Which first or last brings certain death to all?
Were there no Hand, indeed, but human Laws
To Cut the Thread of our Mortality,
Then we'd cause for Grief; but when we reflect
We only leap th' Abiss a little sooner,
Where all Menkind must follow by degrees,
The apprehension moves not me.

Pisante. Oh! Noble Constancy ——
After Ages shall Record the Story,
And Rank thee with the bravest *Roman* Youths;
And Melancholly Virgins when they Read,
In moving accents celebrate thy Name.

Cler. What baleful Planet Rul'd when thou wert Born,
That mark'd for thee this path of Sorrow out?
Oh! ye malicious Stars, when ye had stood
So long the rude buffets of blind Fortune,
And now just as the pleasing Scene appear'd,
I'th' moment when th'art found of Noble Birth,
And Wed to thy long wish'd for Bride *Lucasia*,
Then to snatch the hence, is twice to kill thee.
Oh! it is the mock'ry of spightful Fates,
When we with Labour reach the aim'd at Wish,
Straight this unstable Fairy World removes,
We dye, or are dash'd back again to what we were.

Enter

Enter Eugenio *and* Lucasia.

Lucasia. Faithful *Iras* how shall I reward thee?
Ha! see where stands *Polante* and his Friend!
Oh! lead me *Irus*, quickly, lead me back,
Else I shall grow a Statue at this sight:
Not all the frightful noise of Chains we've past,
And Meagre Looks of Wretches in Dispair,
Are half so terrible as this.

Palante. My *Lucasia!*
Art thou come to take thy last adieu, and
Bless my Eyes before they close for ever?

Luc. Oh! *Palante!*

Pal. What! no more? Give thy labouring Sorrows vent,
That like Convulsions heaves thy Snowy Breasts,
And struggles for a passage to thy Tongue.

Luc. Oh! I had dy'd ere seen this fatal Hour,
But this good Man persu'd with Care my steps,
And stopt my Hand, which else had giv'n the blow,
When first I heard the sad and dreadful News,
That thou, *Palante*, wer't Condemn'd to Dye

Eug. Still all I ask is, that you woud have patience,
I'll to Court where Lord *Euphenes* is,
Now begging for his Son, in hope to bring you happiness.
[*Exit Eug.*

Luc. Fly *Irus*, fly, and bring us instant word.
Oh! my aking Brain is near distraction;
For much I fear there is no help for me.

Pal. Yet I rejoyce in this, I'm found of Noble Birth ——
That in succeeding Ages, when this Act,
With all its Circumstances shall be told
No blot may rest upon thy Virgin Fame;
No censuring Tongue reflect upon thy Choice;
And say, thy Husband was a wretch unknown,
And quite unworthy of *Lucasia*'s Arms.

Luc. What Comfort's in this late discovery found?
Will the Greatness of thy Race protect thee?
Virtue and ev'ry Good was thine before,
Yet the Cruel Pow'rs are deaf to all my Prayers:
Nor will thy Merit plead with angry Heav'n,
To ward the stroak, and save thy precious Life.
Oh Greatness! thou vain and vap'rish shew,
That, like a Mist, dazzles the Eyes of Men,
And as the Foggs destroy the Body's Health,
That Poisons deep, and Gangers in the Soul;
But seldom's found t'assist the Virtuous Man.
Thou wert ——
As dear to these desiring Eyes before;
And honour'd full as much in this poor Heart.
Oh! I cou'd Curse the separating Cause,
And wish *Lucasia* never had been Born.

Pal. Be calm, my Love, my everlasting Dear,
Cease to Lament, and give thy Spirits ease.
Oh! hear me Heav'n, and grant my last Request;
May Health, long Life, and ev'ry Bliss beside,
Conduce to make *Lucasia* happy still
Let nothing fall to interrupt her Joy,
But make it Lasting as you make it Great.
Grant this, and I to rigorous destiny
Submit with pleasure.

Luca. Long Life, no, rather wish me sudden Death,
To rid me of my Cares, and that way give me ease.
Ha! I'm seiz'd with an unusual terror, Fear
And Horrour swim in shades of Night around,
How sad and dreadful are these Prison Walls!
Thy Voice seems hollow too, and Face looks pale.
Oh! my *Palante*, my Heart——
Throbs, as if the Strings of Life were breaking.
[A Bell Tolls within.
Hark! hark! Oh! 'twas this that it foretold.
Ope' Earth, hide me in thy unfathom'd Womb,
To Drown the call of Fate——this dismal Bell.

Cler. Madam——
Be patient, add not to his Misery;
For whilst he sees you thus, his Soul's unfit
For ought but Earth; th' approach of Death is near,
A little time is necessary now,
To calm his Mind to suffer like a Man.

Luc. Oh! Heav'n help me. *[Faints.*
Pal. Oh! She's dying; do not thus rend my Soul with Grief.

Enter an Officer.

Officer. Gentlemen, this Bell gives warning, that within
Half an hour you must prepare to dye.
Palan. 'Tis very well, we shall be ready.
Canst thou conduct this Lady to her Father's House?
Luc. Stand off, and touch me not. No, I will stay with thee.
Do not push me from thee, my Dear *Palante*,
For I shall dye apace, and go before.

Officers.

Officers. The Officers all wait to Conduct ye to the Place of Execution.

Cler. We come now, Friend, when shall we meet again.

Pal. The bless'd Pow'rs can tell, in Heav'n sure.

Lac. Oh! all ye Maids that now are crown'd above;
Did any feel, like me, the Wracks of Love?
By Tempests torn from my dear Husband's Side,
And made a Widdow, when I'm scarce a Bride.

SCENE the Governour's House.

Enter Governour and Count Virro, *and Lord* Granvelle.

Gover. This is strange *Palante* should be found
The Lord *Euphenes* Son; but fear not Nephew, the Law has Pass'd and he shall suffer.

Virro. I urge it still, my Lord, she was my promised Wife;
Her Father so design'd her, had he then been known
Euphenes Son. I urge that, speak my good Father.

Granv. My Lord, I had; yet let me own, I rather wish the unknown *Palante*, had suffer'd for my Daughter, than the Son of one, who tho' my Foe, I must acknowledge Great and Brave.

Gover. So wou'd I, my Lord, but there's no Fence for Accidents; I do expect to be beset with Prayers and Tears, but all in vain, see where he comes.

Enter

Enter Euphanes *and* Alphonso.

Euph. Behold! Lord Gover. my aged Knees, are bent to thee, 'Tis in thy Power to wrest this heavy Judgment of the Law; Suspend it at least, till the King shall hear the Cause, And save my Son.

Gover. Rise *Euphenes*, your Speech carries a double Meaning, you Pray and Threaten with the same Breath, we are not to be frighted Lord, the Laws of *Sicily* have had their Course, your Son falls by them.

Euph. Oh! mistake me not, I am as Humble as your Pride can wish me, but give me leave to speak tho' 'Tis my hard Fortune to offend, let me the anguish of my Soul deliver to that inju ious Lord, the Father of *Lisander*'s, or by the more known Name, *Palante*'s Wife; Hard-harted Man! had'st thou no other Way to wreke thy Caneard and long foster'd Hate upon my Head, but this? Thus cruelly, by my Son's Suffering, and for such a Fault as thou shou'dst Love him, rather? Is thy Daughter injur'd by this Marriage? Is his Blood base? Or can his now rising Fortunes know an Ebb? This Law was made to restrain the Vile from wronging noble Persons, by Attempts of such a kind; but where Equality meets in the Match, the e is no Crime; or if there is, forgive his Youth, and have pity on him.

Gov *Euphenes*, you wrong your Virtue when you'd save a Criminal; the Law condemns, tho' the righteous Judgment falls upon your Son, and your Appeal shall come too late.

Euph.

Euph. Then you have set a Period to a Loyal House and Family, that have been Props of the *Sicilian* Crown, and with their Blood in Wars, won many an honour'd Field.
I can spend no more in Tears, I'll spend the sad Remnant of my childless Age, and only wish to rest i'th' Grave together.

Alph. Hear me thou Governour, not kneeling, but erect as old Age and Slavery has left me: This noble *Sicilian* Youth was lost in defending *Sicily* from the fam'd Fortress, which beat back a Thousand Times, invading Foes, and sunk 'em in the working Seas, from thence the Child was ta'n, and must he 'scape the hazzards of the rowling Waves, Rocks, Tempests, Pirates, and ignominious Fate, to perish in his Native Isle: Oh! barbarous Usage, stop yet at least his Judgment, and let this poor old Man see once again, his dear *Palante*; for that I'll bow my stubborn Knees, and ask the Blessings as I importune Heaven.

Euph. Oh! my Lord, let my unhappy Son appear before ye, e'er the cruel Sentence comes to Execution.

Gran. If you deny them this, it may be ill represented to the King.

Virro. I fear, my Lord, you are Staggering.

Gov. Nephew, be silent, and be safe; they shall have their Will, but to no purpose, only a Moments short delay; for I have sworn, and he shall dye——Guard, bring here the Prisoner.

Euph. I thank the Governour.

Gov. Oh spare thy Thanks, till thou hast real Cause; the Law, the Statutes plain, and he must die for't, there is no Remedy.

Enter

Enter, brought in by the Guards, Palante, Clerimont, Lucasia *and* Eugenio.

Euph. Oh! Son!
Alph. Palante!
Pal. Pardon me, Sirs, I have too much of Tenderness upon my Soul already, too many Clogs that drags it downwards, oh! forgive me, if I beg ye wou'd not add more Weight to Death.

Gra. Madam, 'twere more becoming to your Quality and Modesty, to be at Home; thou do'st but ill Return thy Father's Care.

Luc. I have no Father, nor ever had that I remember, but born and destin'd for an out-cast Wretch, and Curs'd to Ruine a most Noble Husband: Oh! he was the Pride of the *Sicilian* Youths, and Glory of the World; but he is dead or doom'd to die, and that's alike destracting.

Euph. Heav'n bless thee, thou Mirrour of thy Sex, that in the Sea of thy Transcendant Vertues, drown'st all thy Father's Malice, and in my Thought, redeem'st more than thy Race can loose.

Gover. Lord *Euphenes,* what end had you in this, in bringing here the Criminals.

Euph. To move your Mercy, was my End, but Wolves and Tigers know not what pity means.

Gover. Forbear reproach, and hear me; I'll stand it to the King, and all the World, here is an Heiress stole, the worst of Robberies; he is Condemn'd by the Law, he fell to the Judgment of the Law; I surrender him. Guards carry on the Pris'ners.

Luca. Oh! cruel Sentence! hear me, *Sir.*
Gover. Away with 'em.

K *Eug.*

Eug. Stay yet a little thou most Imperious Governour; for I will be heard.

Gov. Thou! What art thou?

Eug. My name is *Irus*, Lord *Pirro* knows me.

Pirro. Ha!

Eug. Thou Tremblest Lord, hear, you that have Condemned these Noble Friends, and hurt their Lives for a meer trifle: Sentence to death a Man for Loving and being beloved, hear, a black deed will start your Souls with Horrour, and make you own the Crime before ye nothing.

Gov. What means the Fellow?

Eug. Nay, 'tis not a Frown can stop me, nor will my Fate be long, know then, this Lord gave out his Son *Eugenio* dy'd at *Rome*, but he was well, and in this City.

Pal. How say'st thou?

Luc. Proceed, dear *Irus*.

Eug. First stop Lord *Pirro*; for my Story will not please him: I say *Eugenio* lived; which when I discover'd to that trembling Lord, he brib'd me with a Thousand Crowns to Poison him. Here's the Agreement under his own Hand; and here's a Letter from *Eugenio* to his Father, which denotes that he was Poison'd, and Dying.

Gra. Let me see it. Oh! 'tis his hand. Wretch that I am, is my dissembled Grief turn'd to true Sorrow. Were my acted Tears but Prophesies of my ensuing Woe? And is he dead! Oh! Pardon me, dear Ghost of my *Eugenio*! 'twas my Crimes that call'd this hasty Vengeance from above, and shorten'd thus thy Life, for whilst with fallacies, I sought to fasten Wealth upon our House, I brought a Cannibal to be the Grave of me and mine; Rase, Bloody Murthering Lord.

Pirro. Vile Cozener, Cheater and Dissembler, now indeed we both are caught.

Euph. Oh! cruel Man! now see the justice of offended Heav'n, Thou who pursu'st the poor *Palante's* Life, with so

much

much Violence, thou now must feel the weight of a Sons loss.

Gov. This will prove a Trajedy indeed; away with the Prisoners, your Trial's next Lord *Pirro*.

Pirro. I do confess———

Eug. Hold, is there no means left to save them? Wou'd not you now Lord *Gravello*, give your Daughter freely to *Palante*?

Gra. More willingly than I wou'd live another Hour.

Euph. Oh! you are kind too late, had you been thus when need required you'd sav'd your self and me, and both our hapless Sons.

Gover. Oh! Nephew, my Prompter still in Cruelty,
Now thou thy self must feel the rigour of the Law

Eug. Now ye behold the good from bad, which naught but this extremity had shewn, yet all be safe, *Eugenio* lives, and fair *Lucasia* is no Heiress now.

Omnes. How! lives!

Eug. Yes, lives to call thee Brother, worthy *Palante*, and thou, my dear *Lucasia*, Sister.   [*Throws off his disguise.*

Luc. Oh! *Irus*, *Eugenio*, *Palante*, where am I?

Palan. Oh! *Lucasia*, *Clerimont*, my Friend, my Love, my Wife.

Eug. Pardon me ye most afflicted Sufferers,
That I thus long have kept my self conceal'd,
My end was honest, to let my Father see
The Frailty, I will not call it by a harder name,
Of Count *Pirro*; the Son he coveted so eagerly,
To raise the Storms to their most dreadful height,
That Calms, and Peace might be more pleasing.

Gra. I see it was *Eugenio*, and thou *Palante*.
Now, my Son, give me thy Hand, here take thy Wife,
And for the wrong that I intended thee, thy Portion shall be double.

Pal. Oh! I am over paid, *Lucasia* and my Friend secure, This is the work of Heav'n, and oh ye gracious Powers I thank ye for it.

Cler. Joy rises from my Heart, and with unutterable Transports stops my Speech; thus once again let me embrace thee.

Euph. And has a Father nothing from the Son?

Alph. And old *Alphonso* too expects a Welcome.

Pal. Oh take me Father, Mother, Friend, *Lucasia*, There's the sum of all.

Luc. Sure such Hours as these gives us a tast of Immortality.

Gra. My Lord *Euphenes*, I hope all Enmity is now forgot betwixt our Houses.

Euph. Let it be ever so, I do embrace your Love. But speak *Eugenio*, What hast thou to ask? Whose timely care prevented our undoing.

Eug. My Lord, you have a Virtuous Neece, for whom I long have sigh'd, I beg your leave to own my Flame.

Euph. She's yours, I've often heard her praise *Eugenio*. And all things else within my power command. My Lord the Governour, you alone seem sad

Gov. I am not so at your good fortune, but that my Nephew whom I have found so base, urg'd me to such cruelty Be gone and hide thy ignominious Head, for I will never see thee more.

Pirro. No matter, I am free, and will enjoy my self in spight of all Mankind.   [*Exit.*

Gov. However this my care shall do, I will solicit earnestly the King to mittigate this cruel Law, and make the Thefts of Love admit of Pardon Who have we here? they seem rejoycing too.

Enter

Enter Larich *Singing,* Francisco, Lavinia, Sancho *and* Trist.

Larich. Ha, hey, what every body injoy! Good News Coz, *Palante* come off safe; my pretty Neece pleas'd here, and Son-in-law, *Francisco,* just receiv'd a certain Information of an Uncle's Death, that has left him, let me see, let me see; ay, ay, enough to please me.

Sancho. Nay, nay, hold, every Body is not so well pleas'd neither; I am Melancholy, I came hither to see the Execution, but I see no Body has occasion to be hanged, but my self, for I have lost my Mistress; Faith, I have *Tristram.* What Account shall I give to my Father of this Match?

Trist. Fackins Master, I cannot tell.

Larich. Then, *Lavinia,* is a Pure Virgin still, for all the Tricks she play'd; Faith she is · was it not a sly one, ha Brother?

Gra. I know nothing of the Matter.

Lu. Cousin, I wish you Joy, as large a Share as I possess, and Fate it self can give no more.

Lav. I am doubly Bless'd to see you Happy.

Fran. And I have nothing left to wish.

Palante. Come my *Lucasia,* now we are Bless'd, let us retire, and give a loose to Raptures yet unknown.

Virtue survives thro' all the Turns of Fate,
Let not impatient Man think Mercy late;
For Heav'n do's still the Justest Side Regard,
And Vertuous Lovers, always meet Reward.

FINIS.

EPILOGUE, Spoke by Mr. *Dogget*.

YOU have seen what Schollar is in Cap and Gown,
   Before his Breedings polish'd by this Town.
'Tis not enough, that he can Hebrew speak,
Greek, Latin, Caldeack, and Arabick,
He may perform his Task in Church and School,
Ne'er drop a Word, that is not Grammar-Rule.
Run through the Arts; can each Degree commence,
Yet be a Freshman still, to Men of Sence.
Tho' the Learn'd Youth, can all the Sages Quote,
Has Homer, Hesiod, and the rest by roat,
Yet what's all this to Picquet, Dress or Play?
Or to the Circle, on a Visiting-Day?
A finish'd Beau, for such fine things I have seen,
That heretofore, has of some Colledge been.
But that Despising, nothing now retains,
For Learning is a Thing requires Brains;
And that's a perquesite the Gentleman disdains.
The Great Dull Ass, from breaking Head of Priscian;
Hither he comes, and writes approv'd Physitian.
The Noise of Chariot brings the Patients in;
Grant them patience, that Physick for their Sin.
Well then——
Since Learning's useless, I'll the Task defie;
Practice, to Ogle, Flatter, Swear and Lye;
For that's the way the Ladies Hearts to gain,
Burn all my Books; my Studies are but vain.
To gain their Looks, each Shape and Dress I'll try;
Smile when they Smile; and when they Frown, I Dye.

BOOKS Printed for, and Sold by WILLIAM TURNER at the Angel, at Lincolns-Inn Back Gate.

THE *English Theophrastus*, or the Manners of the Age, being the Modern Characters of the Court, the Town and the City, written by several Hands, Price Five Shillings.

Letters of Wit, Politicks and Morality, by Cardinal *Bentivoglio*, Father *Rapin*, *Aurelian* the Emperor, Queen *Zenobia*, *Don Quevedo*, *Petronius*, Madam *Maintenon*, &c with several Original Letters of Love and Friendship, by Mr. *Cheek*, Mr. *Savage*, the Senr *Boyer*, Capt *Ayloff*, Mis *Curol*, and several Others, Price Five Shillings.

The *French Spy*, being the Memoirs of *John Baptist*, *De la Fortune*; containing many Secret and Pleasant Transactions, relating both to *England* and *France*, Price Five Shillings.

The Vanities of *Philosophy* and *Physick*, to be perused chiefly by all that would preserve Heath, and prolong Life, as well in a Regular as Irregular Way of Living, by Directions and Medecines therein mentioned, the Third Edition, by Dr. *Gideon Harvey*, Price Five Shillings.

The *Good Old Way* Or Three Brief Discourses, tending to the Promotion of Religion, and the Glory, Peace and Happiness of the Queen and Her Kingdoms, in Three Essays, by *Joshua Barnes*, Her Majestys Greek Professor of *Cambridge*, Price Two Shillings.

Serious Thoughts, on Second Thoughts, being a plain Confutation of Dr *Coward's* Damnable and Erroneous Book, wherein he Endeavours to prove the Opinion of the Souls Existance, to be a plain Heathenish Invention, and not Consonant to the Principles of Philosophy, Reason, or Religion, with a Character of the Dr. Price Two Shillings.

Love at a Loss, or most Votes carry it A Comedy.

The Unhappy Penitent A Tragedy—both written by Mr. *Trotter*.

The Beau Defeated, or the Lucky Younger Brother. A Comedy

Antiochus the Great, or the Fatal Relapse. A Tragedy—by Mrs. *Wiseman*.

Queen Catharine, or the Ruines of Love, by Mrs *Pix*.

Lightning Source UK Ltd.
Milton Keynes UK
UKOW041347080212

186889UK00002BA/54/P